I0755873

3:16

3:16

Meditating through the Bible

DAVID SIMMONDS

RESOURCE *Publications* • Eugene, Oregon

3:16
Meditating through the Bible

Resource Publications
An Imprint of Wipf and Stock Publishers
199 W. 8th Ave., Suite 3
Eugene, OR 97401

www.wipfandstock.com

PAPERBACK ISBN: 978-1-6667-3189-7
HARDCOVER ISBN: 978-1-6667-2492-9
EBOOK ISBN: 978-1-6667-2493-6

. OCTOBER 11, 2021 4:47 AM

This book is dedicated to the memory of the two pastors who each had a formative influence on my Christian discipleship and development.

Both Rev. Douglas McBain ("Mac") and Rev. Michael Wood ("Mike") devoted themselves to serving in Streatham Baptist Church, London ("Lewin") for a combined period of over 30 years whilst I was a young Christian. They were both able to provide regular, systematic, and Biblical teaching - both during Sunday morning and evening services - as well, as mid-week meetings and teaching materials. These two men had a thorough grasp of the Scriptures, as well as practical application to the normal Christian life.

I am indebted to them.

This, you see, is how much God loved the world: enough to give his only, special, son, so that everyone who believes in him should not be lost but should share in the life of God's new age.

John 3:16 (BfE)

Well . . . just think about it!

I will sing to the LORD all my life;

I will sing praise to my God as long as I live.

May my meditation be pleasing to him,

as I rejoice in the LORD.

Ps 104:33–34 NIV

If you know how to worry, you know how to meditate! All you need to do is change what you think about, and you will be practising Christian meditation.

'Meditation' means what you think about, what you allow your mind to dwell on. Your actions and your words are vital. But it is not just your actions and words that can please the LORD or not; it is your inward and unseen meditation as well.

The psalmist praises God for the entire created universe. He says, 'I will sing to the LORD all my life'. Then, he prays, 'May my meditation be pleasing to him'.

What does this mean practically? The apostle Paul has some good advice:

'Whatever is true, whatever is noble, whatever is right, whatever is pure, whatever is lovely, whatever is admirable – if anything is excellent or praiseworthy – think about such things.''

Phil 4:8 BiOY

Acknowledgments

AMP Scripture quotations marked (AMP) are taken from the Amplified Bible, Copyright © 1954, 1958, 1962, 1964, 1965, 1987 by The Lockman Foundation. Used by permission.

BiOY The Bible in One Year app is part of Alpha International. Alpha International is a charity registered in England & Wales (no. 1086179) and in Scotland (no. SC042906) and a private company limited by guarantee and registered in England & Wales (no. 4157379). The registered office is at HTB Brompton Road SW7 1JA.

BiOY – Gumbel, Nicky. London: Hodder & Stoughton, 2019

BfE The Bible for Everyone: Scripture quotations [marked BfE] are reproduced from The Bible for Everyone, copyright © John Goldingay and Nicholas Thomas Wright 2018. Used by permission of the Society for Promoting Christian Knowledge, London, UK. All rights reserved.

BSB The Holy Bible, Berean Study Bible, BSB Copyright ©2016, 2020 by Bible Hub Used by Permission. All Rights Reserved Worldwide.

CEV Scripture quotations marked (CEV) are from the Contemporary English Version Copyright © 1991, 1992, 1995 by American Bible Society. Used by Permission.

CSB Scripture quotations marked CSB have been taken from the Christian Standard Bible®, Copyright © 2017 by Holman. Used by permission. Christian Standard Bible® and CSB® are federally registered trademarks of Holman Bible Publishers.

ERV Taken from the Holy Bible: Easy-to-Read Version (ERV), International Edition © 2013, 2016 by Bible League International and used by permission.

EXB The Expanded Bible: Scripture taken from The Expanded Bible. Copyright ©2011 by Thomas Nelson, Inc. Used by permission. All rights reserved.

ICB Scripture taken from the International Children's Bible®. Copyright © 1986, 1988, 1999 by Thomas Nelson. Used by permission. All rights reserved.

KJV The King James Version is in the public domain.

MSG Scripture quotations marked MSG are taken from THE MESSAGE, copyright © 1993, 2002, 2018 by Eugene H. Peterson. Used by permission of NavPress, represented by Tyndale House. All rights reserved.

NCB Scripture taken from The New Catholic Bible®. Copyright © 2019 Catholic Book. Used by permission. All rights reserved

NIRV Scripture quotations marked (NIrV) are taken from the Holy Bible, New International Reader's Version®, NIrV® Copyright © 1995, 1996, 1998, 2014 by Biblica, Inc.® Used by permission of Zondervan. All rights reserved worldwide. www.zondervan.com The "NIrV" and "New International Reader's Version" are trademarks registered in the United States Patent and Trademark Office by Biblica, Inc.®

NIV Scripture quotations marked (NIV) are taken from the Holy Bible, New International Version®, NIV®. Copyright © 1973, 1978, 1984, 2011 by Biblica, Inc.® Used by permission of Zondervan. All rights reserved worldwide. www.zondervan.com The "NIV" and "New International Version" are trademarks registered in the United States Patent and Trademark Office by Biblica, Inc.®

NLT Scripture quotations marked (NLT) are taken from the Holy Bible, New Living Translation, copyright ©1996, 2004, 2015 by Tyndale House Foundation. Used by permission of Tyndale House, Carol Stream, Illinois 60188. All rights reserved.

INTRODUCTION

IT HAS OFTEN BEEN said that the most famous verse in the Bible is John chapter 3 verse 16. Indeed, many Christians are able to quote it by heart. However, if we asked them about John 3:15 or 3:17, they might struggle.

Not so long ago, I stumbled across 1 John 3:16, and was surprised to find the many similarities with its more famous 'twin'. And then, whilst on a different search, I enjoyed the extraordinary richness and depths to be found in 1 Tim. 3:16 and 2 Tim. 3:16. At which point, I wondered whether something remarkable was occurring. Was there really something special about the 3:16s? Naturally, my first reaction was to discount such a notion. After all, somebody had inserted the chapters and verses long after the canon had been selected and written down. But then I considered, surely all truth is God's truth, and there is an integrity and a cohesiveness throughout the scriptures.

And so began my quest. What about looking at all the 3:16s in the whole Bible? I looked at a few verses at random, and then decided to begin at the beginning with Genesis. I very nearly abandoned the whole project, right there! How could I, a man, dare to comment on such a perilous range of topics and issues as contained in that one verse?

Nevertheless, I prayed and felt the LORD encourage me to spend time meditating on the spread of the Bible, looking at the 3:16 in each book in turn, slowly, deliberately, and carefully. It was then that I became excited to uncover the riches and glories of God as revealed in His Word. The Holy Spirit began to reveal things to me that I had not known or understood before.[1]

> You should meditate . . . by actually repeating and comparing oral speech and literal words of the book, reading and re-reading them with diligent attention and reflection, so that you may see what the Holy Spirit means by them. [2]

BIBLE MEDITATION

> Keep this Book of the Law always on your lips; meditate on it day and night, so that you may be careful to do everything written in it. Then you will be prosperous and successful. Josh 1:8 NIV

> The more you read the Bible; and the more you meditate on it, the more you will be astonished with it.[3]

I have been meditating on the scriptures for many years. Bible meditation is nothing like that of Eastern religions. Instead, it is an opportunity for us to focus on God and concentrate on His Word. Jesus is the living Word of God, and the Bible points us, above all, to the Father, the Son, and the Holy Spirit.

Bible meditation means to take a very short passage or – as in my case – just one verse, and to think about it. I prefer silence, and somewhere calm and alone, with no distractions. Personally, as I meditate on the verse, I find that God speaks to me, and I like to write down what He says on just two pages of a little notebook.

It doesn't happen every day, but regularly and frequently. It is a discipline, and a matter of self-control, which can be helpful as we walk with God through our busy lives. So much is offered,

1. In order to add clarity, and to help you the reader to research further, I have deliberately omitted any page references from the footnotes. Quotations are taken from the relevant '3:16' sections of the works listed in the bibliography.

2. Luther, *The Complete Works of Martin Luther.*

3. Spurgeon. www.spurgeon.org

or demanded, instantly. However, it is sometimes good to enjoy the subtle tastes and textures of a slow-cooked meal rather than the same-old fast food. It is the same with the Bible; it is beneficial for us to slow down and to taste and see what the LORD is saying in just one short part of the Bible, rather than rushing through it, particularly if it is a famous or a favorite passage.

Chapters and verses

> You are well aware, dear friends, that the division into chapters has only been made for convenience' sake and is not a matter of inspired arrangement. I may add that it has been clumsily made, and not with careful thoughtfulness, but as roughly as if a woodman had taken an axe and chopped the book to pieces in a hurry. [4]

The chapter divisions commonly used today in Bibles everywhere were developed by Stephen Langton, an Archbishop of Canterbury. Langton put the modern chapter divisions into place in around A.D. 1227.

Copies of the Latin Vulgate version and the Wycliffe English Bible of 1382 were among the first Bibles to use this chapter pattern. Since the Wycliffe Bible, nearly all Bible translations have followed Langton's chapter divisions.

The Hebrew Old Testament was divided into verses by a Jewish rabbi by the name of Nathan in A.D. 1448. Robert Estienne, who was also known as Stephanus, was the first to divide the New Testament into standard numbered verses, in 1555. Stephanus essentially used Nathan's verse divisions for the Old Testament. Since that time, beginning with the Geneva Bible, the chapter and verse divisions employed by Stephanus have been accepted into nearly all the Bible versions.

However, the ancient Hebrew and Greek styles of grammar, sentence construction, and punctuation are nothing like those of modern English. So, it is often difficult to know where a particular thought or phrase should begin or end.

4. Spurgeon. www.spurgeon.org

For example, in the Tanach (Hebrew Bible) the first verse of each Psalm comprises what, in many English Bibles, would be the heading. For example:

Ps 23 :1 A psalm by David
:2 Hashem is my shepherd; I shall not lack.

All of this has proved difficult for us in the twenty-first century, when we are reading a passage and find that something spills over into the next sentence or even the next chapter.

Bible translations

> He took her by the hand and said to her, *Talitha koum*! (which means Little girl, I say to you, get up!) Mark 5:41 NIV

> Taking hold of the girl's hand, he said to her, *Talitha, koum*! (This means in Aramaic, the language Jesus commonly spoke, Little girl, I tell you to stand up!) Mark 5:41 EXB

> The Aramaic word *talitha* can also mean little lamb. The Greek word used here is *korasion*, which may be a hypocorism, similar to sweetheart. The tenderness of this moment is obvious in the text. However, some Hebrew scholars find in the word *talitha* a Hebrew root that could point to the tallit, or prayer cloak of Jesus, which he may have placed over the girl. This would make his words to mean, Little girl under the prayer cloak, arise. This fringed tallit had already been touched by a woman who received her healing previously in this chapter. TPT

> If you translate the Bible, you are liable to be cross-examined by anybody; because everybody thinks he knows already what the Bible means. [5]

I have decided to only use the order and selection of the traditional and most widely used canonical books of the Bible, rather than to include the apocryphal literature.

5. Knox, *Holy Bible*.

Sometimes, the lyrical qualities of, say, the Authorised Version gives a verse special meaning, whereas on other occasions it is good to be startled by a new paraphrase such as The Message. I have found The Passion Translation refreshing in its style, authority, and approach.

I think it is good to find a version of the Bible that we like, and are familiar with. Some people write in the margins of their Bible specific prayers or comments, which they later read again and find comfort and encouragement. Alternatively, it is also good on occasions to engage with the Living Word in an unfamiliar translation, so that we can receive something fresh from God. A parallel bible can be helpful, too.

I have deliberately used a wide selection of different translations of the Bible in this book, in order to offer us greater understanding of the verses.

Contexts

> Prove all things; hold fast that which is good. 1 Thess 5:21 KJV

> The Bereans are models of right-minded followers. Though zealous to hear, they did not thoughtlessly or uncritically accept what Paul said. They first tested it for themselves from the Scriptures and then submitted themselves to following it. Pursuing this course avoids the potentially disastrous 'blind leading the blind' syndrome.'[6]

It is very important to view a verse or short passage in its wider context. So much of the Bible has been taken by people and used in everyday language. I'm sure we all know someone who has used a Bible verse out of context, in order to prove a point. We may even have done it ourselves!

So we need to firstly read round a verse, to see the wider picture. We need secondly to find out if the rest of the Bible says

6. https://www.bibletools.org/index.cfm/fuseaction/Topical.show/RTD/CGG/ID/1478/Testing-Scriptures.htm

the same thing. Unfortunately, there are many mysteries and paradoxes in the scriptures. So many controversies have been caused by the wrong interpretation of, say, just one word used by Paul on just one occasion in the whole Bible.

It's important to remember that the Bible is a collection of many different books, written over many centuries, written in different styles, and written by many different people.

So ask God for His understanding, His wisdom, and His meaning.

Commentaries

> For we have the living Word of God, which is full of energy, and it pierces more sharply than a two-edged sword. It will even penetrate to the very core of our being where soul and spirit, bone and marrow meet! It interprets and reveals the true thoughts and secret motives of our hearts. Heb 4:12 TPT

> You will need to be familiar with the commentators: a glorious army, let me tell you, whose acquaintance will be your delight and profit.[7]

Preachers, priests, ministers, and pastors all spend time every week commenting to their congregations about the Bible. Learned scholars and academics earn a living by lecturing their students about the Bible. And many others have published millions of books and blogs about the Bible.

It has been both delightful and daunting to sift through just a tiny portion of all these commentaries to distil something new and fresh for us. I have enjoyed learning for myself the new things that God has said through others better equipped than myself.

Again, I have chosen a wide range of different writers and speakers in order to assist us in our meditations.

If we disagree with the commentators, then so much the better. What is the Holy Spirit saying?

7. Spurgeon. www.spurgeon.org

Reflections

> He said to them, This is what I told you while I was still with you: Everything must be fulfilled that is written about me in the Law of Moses, the Prophets and the Psalms. Then he opened their minds so they could understand the Scriptures. Luke 24:44–45 NIV

> The Hebrew word for 'meditate' means to be intense in the mind. Meditation without reading is wrong and bound to err; reading without meditation is barren and fruitless.[8]

It is good to think. Sometimes we're so busy and wondering how we are going to cope with the pressures of life, that we rush from one crisis or problem to another, without giving ourselves time to reflect.

I remember on many occasions encouraging managers to take time to think. It doesn't need to be for very long, but it can prevent merely repeating the same mistakes. It can also help us to do again those things that were really successful.

Pondering on a verse written in the Bible is a wonderful opportunity to get closer to its author! Considering the scriptures helps us to encounter the Living Word of God afresh.

I have included in these sections my own reflections. Obviously, they may not be the same as yours, or of anyone else. But I share with you what I believe the LORD has said to me through the Bible, in the hope that they may be helpful.

More importantly, what is the Holy Spirit saying?

Applications

> Don't just listen to the Word of Truth without responding to it, for that is the essence of self-deception. So we should always let his Word become like poetry, written, and fulfilled by our lives!

8. Watson. https://www.christianquotes.info/quotes-by-topic/quotes-about-meditation/

If you listen to the Word and don't live out the message you hear, you become like the person who looks in the mirror of the Word to discover the reflection of his face in the beginning. You perceive how God sees you in the mirror of the Word, but then you go out and forget your divine origin. Jas 1:22–24 TPT

> To learn and not to do, is really not to learn. To know and not to do, is really not to know.[9]

It's important to meditate with our Bibles open, our minds open, and our notebooks open.

The application sections for each meditation are deliberately blank. They have been left for you to complete. It's vital that we don't just think about the Bible, and know it, and even learn by heart. What God is interested in is that we apply the truths He offers to us in a meaningful way to our lives.

A few years ago, as my wife and I went around the world for a whole year, we believe that God taught us to ask Him: Where do you want us to go, today? Who do you want us to meet, today? What do you want us to say, today?

So . . . stop . . . take three deep breaths .. and in the light of what the LORD has said to you through the Bible, ask yourself what you are going to do, today:

9. Covey, *7 Habits of Highly Effective People.*

Genesis 3:16

Then to the woman He said:

'Let the pain of child-bearing increase

The agony, labor, and stress;

You'll desire a man to control

But find yourself under his rule.'[1]

CONTEXT

It was not until the prospect of victory had been presented, that a sentence of punishment was pronounced upon both the man and the woman on account of their sin.

> Whenever you fall away from Him, God comes searching for you, wanting the relationship to be restored. BiOY

> Perhaps the sentence of 3:8-19 is heavy. But it is less than promised, less than legitimate. The miracle is not that they are punished, but that they live . . . God's grace is given in the very sentence itself . . . Perhaps 'by one man came death' (Rom. 5:12). But the news is that life comes by this one God (cf. John 6:68-69). The sentence is life apart from the goodness of the garden, life in conflict filled with pain, with sweat, and most interestingly, with the distortion of desire.[2]

1. Pawson, *Unlocking the Bible.*
2. Brueggermann, *Genesis.*

God acts and speaks; man rebels; God punishes; God protects and reconciles.[3]

COMMENTARY

We have here the sentence passed on the woman for her sin. She is here put into a state of sorrow, of which only one detail is mentioned, that of childbearing; but it includes grief and fear . . . The punishment was not a curse to bring her to ruin, but a discipline to bring about repentance.[4]

Theologically it is crucial to realize that this passage is not God's last word on gender relations. As Christians we confess that we are no longer under judgment; because of Christ's sacrifice, the judgment has been lifted. We are called to live as new creatures, empowered by the Holy Spirit, submitting to one another.[5]

When sin has the upper hand in woman, she will desire to overpower or subdue or exploit man. And when sin has the upper hand in man, he will respond in like manner and with his strength subdue her, or rule over her . . . 3:16 is the ugly conflict between the male and female that has marked so much of human history. Maleness as God created it has been depraved and corrupted by sin. Femaleness as God created it has been depraved and corrupted by sin. The essence of sin is self-reliance and self-exaltation. First in rebellion against God, and then in exploitation of each other.

So the essence of corrupted maleness is the self-aggrandizing effort to subdue and control and exploit women for its own private desires. And the essence of corrupted femaleness is the self-aggrandizing effort to subdue and control and exploit men for its own private

3. Hamilton, *Book of Genesis chs.* 1-17.

4. Henry, *Commentary to the Whole Bible in One Volume.*

5. Kroeger and Evans, *Women's Bible Commentary.*

> desires. And the difference is found mainly in the different weaknesses that we can exploit in one another.[6]

> The sentence upon the woman gratifies her desire, but crosses it with sorrow. The penalty brings also its blessing; and the blessing its discipline.[7]

REFLECTIONS

In becoming the mother of my children, my wife suffered greatly throughout each pregnancy. But fairly soon after the delivery of each child, the misery was quickly forgotten because of the joy of having this amazing new life in her arms. Jesus said: Just like a woman giving birth experiences intense labor pains in delivering her baby, yet after the child is born, she quickly forgets what she went through because of the overwhelming joy of knowing that a new baby has been born into the world. And Paul writes: Yet a woman shall live in restored dignity by means of her children, receiving the blessing that comes from raising them as consecrated children nurtured in faith and love, walking in wisdom.

One of the most amazing things that Jesus accomplished when He walked on the earth was to turn on its head the historic prevailing attitudes towards women. He is still challenging our notions today concerning the least, the last, and the lost.

What is the Holy Spirit saying?

6. https://www.desiringgod.org/messages/manhood-and-womanhood-conflict-and-confusion-after-the-fall

7. Cambridge Bible for Schools and Colleges http://biblehub.com/commentaries/genesis/3-16.htm

APPLICATIONS

Exodus 3:16

Now be on your way. Gather the leaders of Israel. Tell them, 'God, the God of your fathers, the God of Abraham, Isaac, and Jacob, appeared to me, saying, I've looked into what's being done to you in Egypt, and I've determined to get you out of the affliction of Egypt. MSG

CONTEXT

It is in this remarkable encounter between God and Moses at the holy place of the burning bush in the desert, that the LORD reveals His identity—I AM WHO I AM, or I WILL BE WHO I WILL BE. God knows all about what is about to happen in Egypt, and so He gives His calling, His vocation, to Moses to fulfil His plans. In His sovereign, omniscient, omnipotent, omnipresent purpose, God gives a mere man the free will to choose to obey.

> God tells Moses that 'IAM WHO I AM' is with him. He is sufficient for all your fears, anxieties and challenges. BiOY

COMMENTARY

> God tells Moses in v. 16 to gather the elders together and give them His words . . . They were men of age, men with wisdom, men who obviously knew more than the younger people. When they received this message, they would then pass it on to their families and friends.

> Moses had been gone 40 years, and even before those 40 years, while in Egypt, they didn't know him well because he lived in the palace. If he gave the message to the people directly, it's quite possible that they wouldn't listen to him. But the elders, they were more likely to hear him and believe his words. Then, the younger people were more likely to listen to their elders.
>
> But the elders first had to have confidence in God, so God points them back to a time when He was actively at work with their fathers.
>
> Before they could have confidence in the God who is, they had to look back to the God who was, and they had to believe.[1]

REFLECTIONS

I have been a Christian for over 45 years, and it still amazes me that God—the creator of the universe, the all-powerful, all knowing, ever-present LORD of all—speaks to me, and that I can hear Him, and then make my (feeble) reply! I have actually heard the audible voice of God on four separate occasions in my life, when He said "David!" and I looked round to see who was calling me. However, most of the time, the LORD speaks to me through the Bible, through circumstances, through the peace of the Holy Spirit, and through the wise counsel of mature Christian friends.

1. https://www.sermoncentral.com/sermons/have-confidence-in-god-bobby-oliver-sermon-on-god-in-control-228666?page=4&wc=800

APPLICATIONS

Leviticus 3:16

The priest is to turn them into smoke at the altar as a meal,
as a gift offering, as a nice smell. BfE

CONTEXT

The temple in Jerusalem was the place of sacrifice. Jews can no longer go there for that purpose. But it was also the place above all of God's presence. That is why Jews go there today. Jesus makes clear that He desires mercy not sacrifices for He gave Himself as a fragrant offering and sacrifice to God. Eph 5:2 NIV

He was sacrificed once for all to take away the sins of many. Heb 9:28 NIV

> The God who is Spirit (Jn.4:24) cannot be worshipped by material agents or means, since He is independent of them. Instead, He desires the love and obedience of His followers, and wishes to have fellowship with them by entering their lives and 'eating' with them (Rev 3:20).[1]

Paul urges us to respond in gratitude: Therefore, I urge you, brothers, in view of God's mercy, to offer your bodies as living sacrifices, holy and pleasing to God—this is your spiritual act of worship. Do not conform any longer to the pattern of this world, but be transformed by the renewing of your mind. Then you will

1. Harrison, *Leviticus*.

be able to test and approve what God's will is—his good, pleasing, and perfect will. Rom 12:1-2 NIV

See also Heb 10

COMMENTARY

> As part of their complicated sacrificial rituals, the ancient Jews were required to give God the fat of the bulls and goats.
>
> In order to offer yourself as a living sacrifice to God, you must be holy. That means that you are set apart. On your own, you have no chance of making that work; but through Christ dying in your place, you can be holy and pleasing to God. This means that you must confess your sins to God, and He will forgive you of all unrighteousness. If you want to have a closer relationship with God, you must resist the devil and draw near to God.
>
> The other part of this that is very important for each of us to understand is that God wants your very best. God desired all of the fat because it was the very best and God desires the best from you. Now, I know what you are thinking. I know that you are saying, Well, I'll never be perfect; but I'm here to tell you that is just an excuse. We should strive to live in the will of God and that starts by presenting yourself as a holy and pleasing sacrifice to God every day.[2]

REFLECTIONS

Offerings, slaughters, and sacrifices are so foreign to modern Western culture. But the Holy Spirit calls us to participate in the LORD's sufferings. I'm not sure I understand what this means. Obviously, I can add nothing to all that He accomplished on the cross for me. However, I do know that He requires from me a sacrifice

2. https://www.sermoncentral.com/sermons/the-hope-that-comes-from-sacrifice-shawn-drake-sermon-on-hope-209948?page=2

of praise, and that there is glory in suffering. One of my favorite Christmas carols 'In the bleak midwinter' was written by the Victorian poet Christina Rossetti. In the final stanza, it tells of how the shepherds and wise men were able the bring gifts and offerings to the baby Jesus, but what about me, poor as I am?

> Yet what I can I give Him: give my heart.

APPLICATIONS

Numbers 3:16

So, Moses listed them, just as the LORD had commanded. NLT

CONTEXT

It's so important to just do what God says. Over 75percent of His will for our lives is already written down, in the Bible.

Jesus emphasizes that those who do His will are counted as His family.

And so Moses did just what he'd been told, and he numbered the Levites.

COMMENTARY

> They were numbered as well as the other tribes; but the enumeration was made on a different principle—for while in the other tribes the number of males was calculated from twenty years and upward, in that of Levi they were counted from a month old and upward. The reason for the distinction is obvious. In the other tribes the survey was made for purposes of war, from which the Levites were totally exempt. But the Levites were appointed to a work on which they entered as soon as they were capable of instruction. They are mentioned under the names of Gershon, Kohath, and Merari, sons of Levi, and chiefs or ancestral heads of three subdivisions into which this tribe was distributed. Their duties were to assist in the conveyance of the tabernacle when the

people were removing the various encampments, and to form its guard while stationary.[1]

REFLECTIONS

All the LORD requires from us is that we listen to His voice, and then to obey His word. Jesus is the Word. When I was young, my mother got us children to undertake various chores around the house. In order to prevent the inevitable squabbles between us about what was 'fair', she instituted a rota system, and the jobs were rotated on a weekly basis. In this passage, Moses carried out God's instructions in conducting not just a census return but a list of duties that would continue even after he had died, and they had entered the promised land of Canaan.

The significance here is that the LORD's commands are very clear. The Ten Commandments were first given to His ancient people Israel, and have now been fulfilled in Jesus, who has made them very plain to us. There is no ambiguity about their meaning. Much of the Bible is enigmatic and mysterious, and rightly so. But His commands are plain for all to see. Our problem is not in understanding, but in obeying. Jesus shows us that the two greatest commands are: 'You must love the LORD God with all your heart, all your passion, all your energy, and your every thought. And you must love your neighbor as well as you love yourself.' Luke 10:27 TPT

My response must never be to question, but always just to obey.

1. https://www.biblestudytools.com/commentaries/jamieson-fausset-brown/numbers/numbers-3.html

APPLICATIONS

Deuteronomy 3:16

But to the Reubenites and the Gadites I gave the territory extending from Gilead down to the Arnon Gorge (the middle of the gorge being the border) and out to the Jabbok River, which is the border of the Ammonites. NIV

CONTEXT

In most areas of life, it is important to establish and maintain boundaries. Just as God told Joshua to go in and possess the land, so He wants us too to expand His kingdom rule and reign into every aspect of our lives.

While Moses is still alive, this conquest of Transjordan in the East is symbolic of the victories to come in Canaan in the West after he has died.

COMMENTARY

> The central affirmation about the land is that it is the gift of God to Israel . . . Israel's existence as a people depends on this land and the grace of God . . . Possession of the land and life in it are, therefore, the gift of salvation.[1]

Organization and structures are very important to any community; to the Christian Church as much as to ancient Israel. It is interesting to discover, however, that

1. Miller, *Deuteronomy.*

> the New Testament does not offer us a clear blueprint for Church organization . . . The New Testament instead points to the on-going activity of the Holy Spirit as the divine sanction for our practices and procedures. Flexibility and willingness to adapt to new circumstances are the characteristics of the Church which truly acknowledges God's authority.[2]

> There is hope in being united. As the Israelites were traveling, some of the Tribes began to receive their inherited land. It would have been easy for those men in those Tribes to settle in their land and not continue on. God told them to stay in the army and after they helped the rest of the Nation conquer their land, they could go home and enjoy their inheritance.[3]

REFLECTIONS

A few years ago, my wife and I were visiting a wonderful Christian community in a former Israeli kibbutz on the banks of the River Jordan near the Sea of Galilee. They were ministering to those who were making their Aliyah—returning from the nations to come and settle in Israel. God gave me a prophetic message for the leaders of the community. He told me that He was calling them to the land; it was a land of promise, and a land to possess, and a land of His presence. Just as the LORD established clear boundaries for His ancient people Israel in the promised land, so He sets clear limits on my life.

There were conflicts, and wars, and battles over those areas 3,000 years ago, and there continue to be struggles in the Middle East today. Similarly, there continue to be battles in my own life today. Jesus says, Follow me. The devil whispers Has God really

2. Payne, *Deuteronomy*.

3. https://www.sermoncentral.com/sermons/5-5-the-hope-that-comes-from-spiritual-warfare-shawn-drake-sermon-on-hope-209954?ref=SermonSeriesDetails

said . . . ? Come Holy Spirit and strengthen me as I try to maintain those boundaries.

APPLICATIONS

Joshua 3:16

Just at that moment, the water stopped flowing. It stood up in a heap a great distance away at Adam. This is a town near Zarethan. The water flowing down to the Sea of Arabah (the Dead Sea) was completely cut off. So the people crossed the river near Jericho. ICB

CONTEXT

There are certain important transitions in our lives when it is vital that we ask God to lead us and guide us, and to make a way for us.

> This was a miraculous crossing-over (abar), which was never used for what happened at the Red Sea, which was a liberation. It therefore implies crossing over a boundary and entering into a new life in the Promised Land. More than that, the crossing marked a decisive transition which involved inheriting (acquiring tenancy rights) and finding 'rest'.[1]

COMMENTARY

> Once the people have been prepared properly and the miracle has occurred, the crossing itself is a simple matter.[2]

1. Hamlin, *Joshua*.
2. Miller, *Joshua*.

> The waters were cut off at Adam, near Zarethan, about 18 miles north of Jericho, where the walls of the cliffs are periodically undercut by the strong spring current, causing parts of the cliffs to fall in and temporarily dam up the river. The 'wonder' is in both the act and the timing of God.[3]

> Is there anything that God cannot do? What will He not do to perfect His people's salvation? When we have finished our pilgrimage through this desert, death will be like this Jordan between us and the heavenly Canaan, but the ark of the covenant has prepared a way through it for us; it is the last enemy that will be destroyed.[4]

REFLECTIONS

One of the names of God is YHWH Perizim—the God of breakthroughs.

God is super-natural. After all, He created nature. Miracles are His inexplicable interventions into our everyday, mortal, finite lives. He does this through nature, in circumstances which are still referred to as 'Acts of God'. And He does it by His Holy Spirit in similarly miraculous ways in our own lives, such as healing, deliverance, and salvation.

3. Foster, *Renovaré Spiritual Formation Bible.*
4. Henry, *Commentary to the Whole Bible in One Volume.*

APPLICATIONS

Judges 3:16

The Israelites begged the LORD for help, and the LORD chose Ehud from the Benjamin tribe to rescue them. They put Ehud in charge of taking the taxes to King Eglon, but before Ehud went, he made a double-edged dagger. Ehud was left-handed, so he strapped the dagger to his right thigh, where it would be hidden under his robes. CEV

CONTEXT

This story almost borders on satirical pantomime, reminiscent of the light operas of Gilbert and Sullivan. It demonstrates how the weak can overpower the strong—a favorite Bible theme.[1]

Once again, the people slipped into disobedience and disaster and cried out to God for a deliverer. BiOY

COMMENTARY

'Upon his right thigh'—this would avert all suspicion. Doubtless the war-cloak was flung in folds over the left shoulder, and Eglon, unaware that the bearer of the tribute was left-handed, would see that the side at which arms were usually worn was covered with a flowing robe, and would not suspect the dagger hidden

1. Niditch, *Judges*.

> at the right side. Daggers were often, however, worn at the right side, when a sword was slung to the left. Amasa fell by a similar act of treachery. Joab, advancing to kiss him, clasped his beard with his right hand, while with his unsuspected left he gave the deadly thrust. [2]

> Now Ehud would have been an unlikely candidate to deliver the people from Eglon's grip because of his disability. The text says that he was a left-handed man, but it literally says, bound or handicapped as to his right hand. For some reason Ehud did not have use of his right hand. Moreover, the Benjamites were known for being ambidextrous, having equal ability with both hands. His visible disability in his right hand and his hidden capability with his left-hand provided the perfect strategy to liberate Israel from the Moabites.
>
> What most people recognize as a weakness can be strong in the hands of God. The enemy overlooked Ehud because it did not seem that he could be a threat. Your enemy may be overlooking some things about you because of your disability; but God can use you to have victory over your enemy.[3]

REFLECTIONS

Some people question the inclusion of such stories in the Bible, with their themes of deviousness and deliverance. But the almost comical—though tragic—details demonstrate the historical truth of the scene. Left-handedness is often viewed by society as a disability, but here it proved an advantage. At school, I was often mocked or bullied for wearing glasses, but in my career I have put my eyesight to great use when been paid to read books and academic journals! Paul clearly says that when I am weak, then I am strong.

2. Ellicott, *Commentary on the Whole Bible vol.* 2.

3. https://www.sermoncentral.com/sermons/the-hope-that-comes-from-your-disability-shawn-drake-sermon-on-hope-209956?page=2

APPLICATIONS

Ruth 3:16

When Ruth went back to her mother-in-law, Naomi asked, What happened, my daughter? Ruth told Naomi everything Boaz had done for her. NLT

CONTEXT

Boaz was a redeemer. This morality story illustrates how Ruth—from Moab—lay defenseless at his feet all night. It was an accepted way that a woman could propose marriage to a man. He covered her with his cloak, and didn't touch her (see Ezek 16:8)—the LORD is the Bridegroom, who covers our vulnerability, gives us His promise, enters into a covenant with us, and takes us as His bride. And then they had a child, called Obed, who would become the grandfather of King David.

COMMENTARY

> Naomi asked her: 'How did you get along? Are you the bride or not? Are congratulations in order?'.[1]
>
> Ruth came for the right purpose, to the right person, having made the right preparations and putting herself in the right place. When we find Ruth at the feet of the LORD of the harvest, this is the turning point of the whole story. From this point on, Boaz is busy. Ruth

1. Henry, *Commentary to the Whole Bible in One Volume.*

> now rests and waits to see what Boaz will do. She trusts his word. Have you come to the feet of the LORD of Harvest? Have you responded to His invitation? We will find no rest until we come to Jesus Christ and submit to His Lordship. This place of submission is the only place where God can begin to put our lives back together again. Let's not rebel or argue with God or worry about the future any longer. Let's cleanse our lives and present ourselves to Christ in humble submission.[2]

REFLECTIONS

In effect, Naomi asked her daughter-in-law: 'Are you his wife or not? Did the scheme succeed?' Ruth's identity changed from being a Moabitess to being a servant, and then to being accepted as Boaz's wife. Ultimately, she was in the generational line that led to Jesus.

We are the Bride of Christ. Once we are sure of our identity in Christ, then it ceases to matter what others think about us.

The confidence of my calling enables me to overcome every difficulty without shame, for I have an intimate revelation of this God. And my faith in him convinces me that he is more than able to keep all that I have placed in his hands, safe and secure until the fullness of his appearing. See 2 Tim 1:12-14 TPT

2. https://www.sermoncentral.com/sermons/the-hope-that-comes-from-your-redeemer-shawn-drake-sermon-on-hope-209957?page=3

APPLICATIONS

1 Samuel 3:16

But then Eli summoned Samuel: Samuel, my son! Samuel came running: Yes? What can I do for you? MSG

CONTEXT

Good people want to know all the will of God, whether it is for them or against them. [1]

Samuel had learnt what to do when he heard his name being called.

So much of our Christian faith and our daily lives is based upon the call of God. He speaks to us directly, through His scriptures, and through the prophetic messages He gives to others. The response should always be one of obedience, and a willingness to serve.

> The LORD called Samuel, revealed Himself to Samuel, and he listened to the LORD. BiOY

COMMENTARY

> As soon as ever he heard Samuel's stirring, he called for him, probably to his bedside. He had reason enough to fear that the message prophesied no good concerning

1. Henry, *Commentary to the Whole Bible in One Volume.*

him, but evil; and yet, because it was a message from God, he could not contentedly be ignorant of it. [2]

There is hope in listening to and obeying God's voice. Sometimes God tells us things that we really don't want to hear. For Samuel, this was definitely one of those times. God told Samuel that the man who had been raising him and teaching him was going to be destroyed. Not only did God tell Samuel this but Eli made Samuel repeat it to him.

I do want us to notice that Eli did not get mad about this. Notice what Eli said, He is the LORD; let him do what is good in his eyes. When God speaks, we need to listen with an open heart. I guarantee that Samuel did not want to hear what God told him; but he still had to listen.

We need to listen with an intent to obey. God knew Eli was going to ask Samuel what He said. It was even harder to repeat what God said to Eli than it was to hear it.

We need to listen with an understanding. Don't forget that it is Almighty God, the Creator of all things that is speaking to us. Whether you like His plan or not, He is still in charge. We need to stop trying to get God to change His plan and start following it.[3]

REFLECTIONS

One of my most vivid memories as a 6-year-old boy was sitting one dark winter's night with other children at the back of an otherwise empty old, cold Anglican church. The vicar was telling us the story about Eli and Samuel, using the latest technology. We watched the pictures projected onto the screen, and then heard the booming voice of God! It was terrifying!

2. Henry, *Commentary to the Whole Bible in One Volume.*

3. https://www.sermoncentral.com/sermons/the-hope-that-comes-from-hearing-god-s-voice-shawn-drake-sermon-on-hope-209958?page=2

I believe that we need to rediscover that same holy fear of an awesome God. Once we hear His voice and listen to His call, we will run to Him, eager to do whatever He wants.

APPLICATIONS

2 Samuel 3:16

Michal's husband, Paltiel, followed them, crying all the way to Bahurim. Finally, Abner said to him, Go back home. So Paltiel went back home.
ERV

CONTEXT

To our modern Western ears, this seems a strange story. When he fled for his life during the endless battles he had with King Saul, David had to leave behind his first wife Michal, Saul's daughter. The King married her off to Paltiel, and David took other wives, including Abigail. However, Michal's brother Ish-bosheth has now taken his father's place and become King of Israel, whilst David is King of Judah. David now wants Michal returned to him, as a sign of the peace between them. Paltiel's public grief is understandable.

COMMENTARY

> I see God restoring to David all of these things he had lost . . . There is hope in God's restoration of lost relationships. Michal, Saul's daughter had been married to David; but when David escaped from Saul, Saul gave Michal to Paltiel as his wife. Again, there had been many years that had passed since David and Michal had been married; but God reunited them.

> God can bring restoration in relationships in our lives that seem like there is no hope.[1]

REFLECTIONS

Intimacy, friendship, love, trust, and many other blessings are bound up in marriage, where feelings and emotions can be shared in honesty and vulnerability. The loss of a spouse—through death or divorce—is perhaps the most devastating of all bereavements. The Holy Spirit promises to be our comforter—our paraclete—in times of great suffering. We can then share that comfort with others.

1. https://www.sermoncentral.com/sermons/the-hope-that-comes-from-restoration-shawn-drake-sermon-on-hope-209959?page=2

APPLICATIONS

1 Kings 3:16

One day two prostitutes came to Solomon and stood before the king.
ERV

CONTEXT

Access to the king is highly controlled. Even Queen Esther would later need to wait to be invited to speak to her husband. King Solomon is also the highest judge in the land, hearing only the most complex cases.

Solomon needed great wisdom in order to fulfil his calling. He had prayed for wisdom. God answered his prayer more than he could ever have asked or imagined.
BiOY

COMMENTARY

Note the right of access on the part of common members of the kingdom to the king's presence.[1]

The king, at the highest rung of the social ladder, is adjudicating an argument between two women who are very close to its lowest rung. They have little to no political, social, or economic capital, even within the narrative itself, where they are never named beyond the first woman and the other woman. Solomon's attention

1. Carson, *New Bible Commentary*.

> is accessible; he attends even to the least powerful in society.[2]

> It is in the knowledge how to risk failure rather than be reduced to impotence, and how to go straight to the heart of a difficulty when the slow, regular approaches of science are impossible, that we recognize what men call a touch of genius, and what Scripture here calls the 'wisdom of God.'[3]

> This story begins by telling us that the problem was between 2 prostitutes. It is surprising that King Solomon would even hear the case of women let alone prostitutes. As the 2 women argued about what was true and what was a lie; King Solomon just listened.
>
> Christians, we live in a similar situation- We are people who do the wrong things, live in unacceptable situations, and battle among ourselves; and yet God the Father still listens to us. Have you ever thought about the fact that sometimes you and another Christian go to God the Father with a disagreement? Each person expects God to rule in their favor. The great part about this is that God is an unbiased judge. God looks at our hearts, not our checkbooks, color of skin, etc . . . This is why each of us should go to God in prayer.[4]

REFLECTIONS

Whether or not this story actually happened in the life of Solomon or not, or was just another part of the folklore of the time in that region, it remains nevertheless an enduring tale of deceit, true love, and amazing discernment, judgment, and wisdom. And now,

2. https://www.workingpreacher.org/commentaries/narrative-lectionary/solomons-wisdom/commentary-on-1-kings-34-9-10-15-16-28

3. Ellicott, *Commentary on the Whole Bible vol.* 2.

4. https://www.sermoncentral.com/sermons/11-11-the-hope-that-comes-from-wisdom-shawn-drake-sermon-on-hope 209960?ref=SermonSeriesDetails

because of the finished work of Jesus' death and resurrection, we can all have free access to the throne room of the King. God says that the fear of the LORD is the beginning of wisdom. Leaders in the Church should be selected because they are known to receive the wisdom of Holy Spirit. We all need to take heed when God tells us to heed of wisdom's guidance:

> Trust in the LORD completely,
> and do not rely on your own opinions.
> With all your heart rely on him to guide you,
> and he will lead you in every decision you make.
> Become intimate with him in whatever you do,
> and he will lead you wherever you go.
> Don't think for a moment that you know it all,
> for wisdom comes when you adore him with undivided devotion and avoid everything that's wrong. Prov 3:5-7 TPT

APPLICATIONS

2 KINGS 3:16

Elisha announced, The LORD says, 'I will fill this valley with pools of water.' NIRV

CONTEXT

It is important to note that Elisha deliberately chooses to worship, and then is able to hear clearly the word of the LORD. And the message he brings is one of hope and of God's eternal love and provision for His people.

COMMENTARY

> Those who expect God's blessings, must dig pools for the rain to fill.[1]
>
> Elisha may perhaps have come to the neighborhood of the army at the instigation of the Spirit of God because the distress of the kings was to be one means in the hand of the LORD, not only of distinguishing the prophet in the eyes of Joram, but also of pointing Joram to the LORD as the only true God. The three kings, humbled by the calamity, went in person to Elisha, instead of sending for him.[2]

1. Henry, *Commentary to the Whole Bible in One Volume.*
2. Keil and Delitzch, *Commentary on the Old Testament.*

What God had them do was very interesting. God told them to dig ditches and that there would be plenty of water for the men and animals. I love that Elisha says that this is an easy thing for God. Notice, that God not only provided water for them; but also gave them victory over their enemy.

When you are struggling spiritually, seek God for direction. He will not just provide for you; but He will give you victory over your enemies.[3]

REFLECTIONS

In 1976, it was one of the hottest summers on record in the UK. A group of us were hiking in Wales, and I helped us all to get hopelessly lost. We were so thirsty. Eventually, we came across a remote farmhouse. Soon we were able to slake our thirst with pints of the purest, coldest water we had ever drunk. It was unforgettable. God promises to send us the fresh, new, life-giving water of the Holy Spirit to quench our thirst. Jesus says:

> Whoever drinks the water I give them will never thirst. Indeed, the water I give them will become in them a spring of water welling up to eternal life. John 4:14 NIV

3. https://www.sermoncentral.com/sermons/the-hope-that-comes-from-god-s-provision-shawn-drake-sermon-on-hope-209961?page=2

APPLICATIONS

1 CHRONICLES 3:16

The next king after Jehoiakim was his son Jehoiachin. After that, Josiah's son Zedekiah became king. NIRV

CONTEXT

> Seldom has a crown gone in direct line from father to son for a total of seventeen generations, as here . . . Of all the families of Israel, none were so illustrious as the family of David: here we have a full account of it. From this family . . . Christ came.[1]

COMMENTARY

For the Jewish nation, names have always held great significance.

> As we read their names they convey no meaning to us, but as defined etymologically we may get a new aspect of part at least of the king's household. Ibhar signifies "God chooseth"; Elishama, "God heareth"; Eliphelet, "God is deliverance"; Eliada, "God knoweth". Keeping in mind the well-established fact that in Oriental countries it was customary to mark family history by the names of the children, we can but be struck with the deep religiousness of the family record now before us. In every child David sees some new manifestation of God. Every

1. Henry, *Commentary to the Whole Bible in One Volume.*

> son was an historical landmark, every life was a new phase of providence. Blessed is the man who need not look beyond his own house for signs and proofs of the manifold and never-ceasing goodness of God.[2]

REFLECTIONS

For many years I have been fascinated by family trees. I have been able to trace the ancestors of both myself and my wife going back 20 generations (although before the early nineteenth century, the facts are not easy to verify!). At the time when this passage was written, oral history was vital to the Israelites. People would learn and recite the stories and genealogies. In this context, 'son' was taken to mean heir, descendent or successor. And 'father' meant a forefather, ancestor, or forebear. All these monarchs were in the kingly line of David that led eventually to our greatest King, Jesus. Paul writes:

> Now if we are children, then we are heirs – heirs of God and co-heirs with Christ, if indeed we share in his sufferings in order that we may also share in his glory. Rom 8:17 NIV

2. Parker, https://biblehub.com/commentaries/illustrator/1_chronicles/3.htm

APPLICATIONS

2 Chronicles 3:16

He made two huge free-standing pillars, each fifty-two feet tall, their capitals extending another seven and a half feet. The top of each pillar was set off with an elaborate filigree of chains, like necklaces, from which hung a hundred pomegranates. He placed the pillars in front of The Temple, one on the right, and the other on the left. The right pillar he named Jakin (Security) and the left pillar he named Boaz (Stability).
MSG

CONTEXT

Solomon builds the temple for the glory of God, following His precise instructions. God has now made us, the people of Christ, into His temple of the Holy Spirit. He calls us to uphold His attributes of security and stability.

COMMENTARY

> Full instructions enable us to go about our work with certainty and to proceed therein with comfort. Blessed be God, the Scriptures are enough to render the man of God thoroughly furnished for every good work. Let us search the Scriptures daily, beseeching the LORD to enable us to understand, believe, and obey his word, that our work and our way may be made plain, and that all may be begun, continued, and ended in him. Beholding God, in Christ, his true Temple, more glorious than

that of Solomon's, may we become a spiritual house, a habitation of God through the Spirit.[1]

There is hope in new beginnings. The pillar named Jakin means, He establishes. When you give your life to Jesus, you begin a brand-new life. It has always been said that it is so much easier to start something new and fresh then it is to try to fix something that is broken. Through the power of the Holy Spirit, you get to start over. In fact, even if you have been a Christian for a long time; you can start new each day. A fresh start to each day should be a pillar in each Christian's life.

There is hope in God's strength. The pillar named Boaz means, In Him is strength. Christians, your strength is found in Christ, not yourself. In the Book of Nehemiah, he says, The joy of the LORD is my strength. Do you want to be strong in the LORD? Do you want to have joy? Through the power of the Holy Spirit, you can have the strength you need to make it through any situation; and you can be joyful throughout the whole thing.[2]

REFLECTIONS

When my wife and I retired, we embarked on a year-long round-the-world adventure with God. As our friends and family asked us how they could pray for us during the year, we just said: All we need is health and safety. Another way of putting it could be Jakin and Boaz—security and stability. They are two great pillars to have in our life. And, yes, Jesus answered those prayers for us

1. Henry, *Commentary to the Whole Bible in One Volume.*

2. https://www.sermoncentral.com/sermons/14-14-the-hope-that-comes-from-god-s-temple-shawn-drake-sermon-on-hope-209964?ref=SermonSeriesDetails

APPLICATIONS

Ezra

My chosen verse ______________________________

The Context

What commentators say

My reflections

My application

Nehemiah 3:16

Nehemiah son of Azbuk ruled half of the district of Beth-Zur, and he rebuilt the next section of the wall. It went as far as the royal cemetery, the artificial pool, and the army barracks. CEV

CONTEXT

Leaders need to get their hands dirty.

> When a general good work is to be done, each should apply himself to that part which is within his reach. If everyone will sweep before his own door, the street will be clean; if everyone will mend one, we shall all be mended. Some that had first done helped their fellows. The walls of Jerusalem, in heaps of rubbish, represent the desperate state of the world around, while the number and malice of those who hindered the building, give some faint idea of the enemies we have to contend with, while executing the work of God. Everyone must begin at home; for it is by getting the work of God advanced in our own souls that we shall best contribute to the good of the church of Christ. May the LORD thus stir up the hearts of his people, to lay aside their petty disputes, and to disregard their worldly interests, compared with building the walls of Jerusalem, and defending the cause of truth and godliness against the assaults of avowed enemies.[1]

1. Henry, *Commentary to the Whole Bible in One Volume.*

COMMENTARY

There is hope in The Holy Spirit. The Fountain Gate appeared to be the gate that was in the worst condition. It was so bad that the ruins of that gate actually blocked Nehemiah's journey when he took a secret tour of the city walls during the night. When he got to the Fountain Gate he had to turn back because he could go no further until it was repaired.

It is believed by many that when the Babylonians attacked Jerusalem; that it was at the Fountain Gate where the main attack took place. This would make sense from a spiritual perspective because it is the True Fountain of Living Water, Jesus Christ; that took the full brunt of the attack from the enemy.

There are a number of places of importance mentioned in the Bible that are associated with the Fountain Gate. Some of these places could only be reached by passing through this gate. The King's Pool, (The Pool of Siloam is where Jesus told the blind man to wash and receive his sight); The King's Garden; The Steps to Zion; The Tomb of David; and The Fountain at the Gihon Spring.

The Fountain Gate got its name from the fact that it was the primary access to the Fountain located at the Gihon Spring. This spring was Jerusalem's only really reliable source of water. In times of drought, the Gihon Spring would still flow freely.

As we go through the Fountain Gate, we find traits of a maturing believer. Without water, you will die. We also need spiritual water flowing through our lives. Let me ask you this morning, What is flowing out of you? See, what is going on around you is not very important compared to what is flowing out of your life. Is what flowing out of you living, dead, or stopped up? A maturing believer allows the Holy Spirit of God to be filled in their life to a point that the Holy Spirit is overflowing from their life.[2]

2. https://www.sermoncentral.com/sermons/the-hope-that-comes-from-jesus-shawn-drake-sermon-on-hope-209965?page=3

REFLECTIONS

As a management development expert, I have led many learning events on themes of leadership and teams. I have drawn heavily on the exceptional model of Nehemiah, in his task of uniting and mobilizing the people of Jerusalem in rebuilding the walls. Nehemiah was a leader who got his hands dirty. It took 52 days for them to make the journey from Babylon back to their Promised Land, and 52 days for them to rebuild the walls. And now Jesus offers us a new model, that of the Servant Leader.

APPLICATIONS

Esther

My chosen verse ___________________________________

The Context

What commentators say

My reflections

My application

Job 3:16

Why was I not buried like a child born dead, like a baby who never saw the light of day? NCV

CONTEXT

Given all his trials and tribulations, it is understandable that Job should demand of God: Why?

Here Job refers back to the 'why' questions of vv. 11-12. The question 'Why?' is perhaps the most common one asked by toddlers, and the most agonizing by distraught adults. And as with Job at the end of the book, God tends not to answer this question.

COMMENTARY

> Why is the human question—universal as well as individual, essential as well as existential. Sometimes it is the question of curiosity, as when a child or a scientist asks why. Sometimes it is the question of doubt, as when satan tempts Eve or the cynic refuses to believe. At other times, as in Job's case, why is a cry of despair arising from an unexplainable contradiction.[1]
>
> A great deal of suffering can be explained as being the result of the fact that we live in a fallen world: a world

1. McKenna, *Communicator's Commentary: Job.*

where all creation has been affected, not only by the sin of human beings, but also by that of satan's sin. BiOY

REFLECTIONS

Many years ago, before I gave my heart to Jesus, I was diagnosed with clinical depression. When I became a Christian, the Father gave me a wonderful picture of His loving hands beneath me. He promised that no matter how dark life became, and no matter how far I fell, He would always be there for me, and He would catch me. Nothing can separate me from His love—not even depression.

APPLICATIONS

Psalms

My chosen verse ________________________________

The Context

What commentators say

My reflections

My application

Proverbs 3:16

Wisdom extends to you long life in one hand and wealth and promotion in the other. TPT

CONTEXT

The words of Christ's Sermon on the Mount in general, and the Beatitudes in particular, contain echoes of much of the truth concerning wisdom and foolishness. Wisdom is a beautiful lady whereas sin is a seductive temptress.

When you find Jesus, you find the source of all wisdom. This is the path of blessing . . . This is the path to long life. BiOY

COMMENTARY

Notice that wealth is held in the left hand. For the Hebrews, the left was the side of lesser worth . . . and even misfortune . . . Even at its most materialistic, wisdom offers a man no encouragement to give his life to making money.[1]

Wisdom can bring long life. Now, this is not a guarantee; but it does make sense. This is saying that with wisdom

1. Aitken, *Proverbs*.

you are not going to have your life cut short through foolish choices and activities.

Wisdom can bring riches and honour. Before we interpret this as we are going to be rich and famous; remember that the riches a Christian is supposed to be storing up is riches in Heaven.

Wisdom leads to pleasant and peaceful paths. Again, this doesn't mean that your life is going to have no troubles. It means that when you apply wisdom to your life that you will find peace and joy in Christ.[2]

REFLECTIONS

Solomon is renowned not for seeking fame and fortune, but for asking God for wisdom. Consequently, God gave him not only the wisdom he had asked for, but the riches and prominence that flowed from it. Jesus wants us to ask Him for the gift of wisdom that comes from the Holy Spirit, and to store up for ourselves treasures in heaven.

2. https://www.sermoncentral.com/sermons/17-17-the-hope-that-comes-from-finding-wisdom-shawn-drake-sermon-on-hope-209967?ref=SermonSeriesDetails

APPLICATIONS

Ecclesiastes 3:16

Everywhere on earth I saw violence and injustice instead of fairness and justice. CEV

CONTEXT

At the time of Noah, there was violence—robbery—throughout the earth. Corruption and bribery are still rampant throughout the world. The lack of justice—particularly for the poor—grieves God's heart.

COMMENTARY

> The Teacher's experience of the world raises fundamental questions about justice. Even though in 2:17 he asserts a traditional belief in God's ultimate reward for the righteous and punishment for the wicked, his later comments . . . show just how difficult it was for him to affirm God's just rule in the world in the light of his experience.[1]
>
> The limits of human intellect and agency address another challenge in verse 16: the reality of wickedness in the place of justice and righteousness. The governmental structures that are supposed to be bulwarks of justice and righteousness have become utterly corrupt, so the poor and weak have no recourse. Wickedness reigns in

1. Foster, *Renovaré Spiritual Formation Bible.*

> the world. Qohelet [The Teacher] refuses to offer an explanation for this distressing state of affairs: in this respect also the world of our experience is absurd. To try to make rational sense of it is to deny its horrors.[2]

REFLECTIONS

This verse could so easily be a summary of today's news. However, since it was written over 2,500 years ago, it shows that the wickedness, violence, injustice, and corruption of mankind and the influence of the devil will continue until the time when Jesus returns in glory to reign over the earth as He does in heaven.

2. Plantinga-Pauw, *Proverbs and Ecclesiastes.*

APPLICATIONS

Song of Solomon

My chosen verse ________________________________

The Context

What commentators say

My reflections

My application

Isaiah 3:16

God says, Zion women are stuck-up, prancing around in their high heels, making eyes at all the men in the street, swinging their hips, tossing their hair, gaudy and garish in cheap jewelry. MSG

CONTEXT

God's people are continually rebellious and unfaithful Him, because of their pride, immorality, and greed.

This prophecy provides an appropriate sequel to the condemnation of the male leaders of society earlier in the chapter, and so applies to all who love ostentation and luxury.

COMMENTARY

> On Mt. Zion was located the ruling class, and the address is to women of this group. Isaiah sees them as vain and indifferent.[1]
>
> Zion is the place where YHWH dwells and reveals himself. The inhabitants of the city, including the women, must be persons fit for that privilege and responsibility. The entire book reflects God's search for a people fit to live in His city in meekness and humility.[2]

1. Brown, *New Jerome Biblical Commentary.*
2. Watts, *Isaiah.*

> The effect of self-exaltation is a confrontation with the only truly self-sufficient Being in the universe, the only One whose glory is not derived.[3]

REFLECTIONS

Earlier in the chapter, Isaiah had remonstrated against the pride and arrogance of the men. And now he turns his attention to the women. In conversation with a good friend of mine, a modern Orthodox Jew, he said that the issue here is not really about gender. These were the educated people of high-standing. They were the self-righteous in society. God hates haughtiness. He so loves those who want to become more like His precious Son, who is gentle and humble in heart. Paul summed it up well:

> Therefore if you have any encouragement from being united with Christ, if any comfort from his love, if any common sharing in the Spirit, if any tenderness and compassion, then make my joy complete by being like-minded, having the same love, being one in spirit and of one mind. Do nothing out of selfish ambition or vain conceit. Rather, in humility value others above yourselves, not looking to your own interests but each of you to the interests of the others. Phil 2:1-4 BSB

3. Oswalt, *Book of Isaiah* 1-39.

APPLICATIONS

JEREMIAH 3:16

And it shall be that when you have multiplied and increased in the land in those days, says the LORD, they shall no more say, The ark of the covenant of the LORD. It shall not come to mind, nor shall they [seriously] remember it, nor shall they miss or visit it, nor shall it be repaired or made again [for instead of the ark, which represented God's presence, He will show Himself to be present throughout the city]. AMP

CONTEXT

The Ark of the Covenant was the most precious article known to God's ancient people Israel, since it signified the place of His presence in the Holy of Holies, initially in the tabernacle and subsequently in the temple. The Ark would later be substituted by Jerusalem itself as the place of God's dwelling.

And now He lives in us.

COMMENTARY

> But in the gospel temple Christ is the ark; he is the propitiatory, or mercy-seat; and it is the spiritual presence of God in his ordinances that we are now to expect. Many expressions are here used concerning the setting aside of the ark, that it shall not come to mind, that they shall not remember it, that they shall not visit it, that none of these things shall be any more done; for the true worshippers shall worship the Father in spirit and in

> truth, Jn. 4:24 . But this variety of expressions is used to show that the ceremonies of the law of Moses should be totally and finally abolished, never to be used any more, but that it would be with difficulty that those who had been so long wedded to them should be weaned from them; and that they would not quite let them go till their holy city and holy house should both be levelled with the ground.[1]

> There is hope in being in God's presence. The Ark of the Covenant represented God's presence and God was telling them that there would be a day that the Ark of the Covenant would not be necessary. The reason for that is Jesus. Through the blood of Jesus Christ, Christians can go into the presence of God anytime.[2]

REFLECTIONS

Over 40 years ago, I really enjoyed the George Lucas film Indiana Jones and the Raiders of the Lost Ark starring Harrison Ford. But instead of seeking the ark, we need to search for the increasing evidence of the Holy Spirit's existence within our hearts. We should pray, as Jesus does:

> for those who will believe in me through their message, that all of them may be one, Father, just as you are in me, and I am in you. May they also be in us so that the world may believe that you have sent me. I have given them the glory that you gave me, that they may be one as we are one. John 17:20-22 NIV

1. Henry, *Commentary to the Whole Bible in One Volume.*

2. https://www.sermoncentral.com/sermons/20-20-the-hope-that-comes-from-god-s-presence-shawn-drake-sermon-on-hope-209970?ref=SermonSeriesDetails

APPLICATIONS

Lamentations 3:16

He made me eat gravel and rubbed me in the dirt. CEV

CONTEXT

In the Middle East, where dough is often baked in the ashes of the fire, the grit may get mixed with the bread. Jesus was clearly thinking of this when describing the love of His heavenly Father. He would never give a stone to His children who ask Him for their daily bread. Instead, He always gives us His Holy Spirit.

COMMENTARY

> The world says, When you hit rock bottom, the only way is up; and there is some truth to that; but the Christian should say, Sometimes God lets you hit rock bottom so that you will discover that He is the Rock at the bottom.[1]

REFLECTIONS

God's discipline is rarely if ever sought. However, He corrects us because of the love He has for us. There have been occasions in my life when—much later—I have looked back and reflected on

1. https://www.sermoncentral.com/sermons/the-hope-that-comes-from-brokenness-shawn-drake-sermon-on-hope-209971?page=1

a situation and given thanks to Jesus that He scolded me and so prevented greater problems.

APPLICATIONS

EZEKIEL 3:16

At the end of the seven days, I received this Message from God MSG

CONTEXT

> He who has been musing and meditating on the things of God all week was ready to hear God speak to him.[1]

The watchman who fails to give warning of approaching danger is personally responsible, but if he gives due warning, then his hearers bear the responsibility themselves if they fail to give it consideration and then take action.

COMMENTARY

> There is hope in the Word of God. Without God's Word, we wouldn't have a clue to what His plan is for our lives. Christians, you cannot grow without the Word of God. I challenge each of you to not just read the Word; but to apply it to every situation you encounter. As you are watching all that happens around you, how does it match up to the Word of God?
>
> There is hope in the work of God. God made Ezekiel a watchman for Israel. Notice, God didn't ask him if he wanted to be a watchman. God told him. This reminds

1. Henry, *Commentary to the Whole Bible in One Volume.*

me of what Jesus told the Disciples as He went into the Garden of Gethsemane.[2]

REFLECTIONS

As with God's precious people Israel, the LORD gives us a choice. We must regularly choose whether to trust or to ignore the sentry's warning, which he had waited for so diligently. Do we want a life with God? As He said through Moses:

> This day I call the heavens and the earth as witnesses against you that I have set before you life and death, blessings and curses. Now choose life, so that you and your children may live and that you may love the LORD your God, listen to his voice, and hold fast to him. For the LORD is your life. Deut 30:19-20 NIV

2. https://www.sermoncentral.com/sermons/22-22-the-hope-that-comes-from-watching-shawn-drake-sermon-on-hope-209972?ref=SermonSeries-Details

APPLICATIONS

DANIEL 3:16

Shadrach, Meshach, and Abednego answered the king, saying, Nebuchadnezzar, we do not need to defend ourselves to you. EXB

CONTEXT

They did not need to defend themselves. It was all just a matter of following the 2nd commandment.

> They need not answer; it is a time for action, not for words; God is able to save them, and in any case they will not obey the king.[1]

> The confrontation between the king and the three Jews is the first of two dramatic high points in the narrative and enables the three to articulate their actions in a confessional statement. The encounter with the ruler later becomes a regular feature of martyr legends.[2]

COMMENTARY

> This is a matter for God, and He will answer with deeds, not words. This type of reply is characteristic of the martyr legends . . . There is a certain pride such as appears again in Daniel's answer to the king . . . a pride growing out of a consciousness that as servants of God

1. Peake, *Commentary on the Bible.*
2. Newsom, *Daniel.*

> they are superior to ant earthly potentate and so have need neither of his clemency nor his gifts.[3]
>
> There is hope in devotion to God. This is definitely something that is missing amongst most Christians today. To be devoted to someone means that you are willing to die before betraying them. Shadrach, Meshach, and Abednego were willing to die before they would bow to anyone besides YHWH God. They didn't have any guarantees that God would save them; but they were still devoted to Him. They simply knew that God was able to save them and that's all they needed. Are you willing to be devoted to God like that? Even if God may not give you what you want?[4]
>
> The concluding words of the three Jews have long been admired, as the storyteller certainly intended, as a defiant statement of uncompromising fidelity to God in the face of terrible threats. What is less often noted is what this stance discloses about the dynamics of power. Their refusal to comply with the king's order, despite the threat of the worst that he can inflict, exposes the limits of dictatorial power. Nebuchadnezzar literally has no power to enforce his command, to make the Jews behave like all the rest of his officials. He can kill the three Jews; but he cannot make them worship his god. Even if they should not be saved, in this matter they have more power than the mighty king of Babylon. The recognition of this unforeseen reversal is what fuels Nebuchadnezzar.[5]

REFLECTIONS

Because this story is so familiar to us, we are in danger of losing the essential message laid out for us. Above all, God honors the

3. Keck, *Interpreter's Bible Commentary.*

4. https://www.sermoncentral.com/sermons/23-23-the-hope-that-comes-from-faithfulness-shawn-drake-sermon-on-hope-209973?ref=SermonSeries-Details

5. Newsom, *Daniel.*

friends' obedience to Him, and their faith in Him. Somebody has said that our walk with the LORD must be in the pair of boots called Trust and Obey.

APPLICATIONS

Hosea

My chosen verse ______________________________

The context

What commentators say

My reflections

My application

Joel 3:16

The sky turns black, sun and moon go dark, stars burn out. God roars from Zion, shouts from Jerusalem. Earth and sky quake in terror. But God is a safe hiding place, a granite safe house for the children of Israel. Then you'll know for sure that I'm your God, Living in Zion, my sacred mountain. Jerusalem will be a sacred city, posted: 'No trespassing.' MSG

CONTEXT

God's final judgment of all nations will be unlike anything the world has ever known.

> The decision of whether or not to call on the name of the LORD has far-reaching implications. BiOY
>
> It will be a terrible day for evildoers . . . it will be a joyful day for the righteous.[1]

COMMENTARY

> Christians at once hope for the eradication of all evil and the salvation of their souls. God is not mocked.[2]
>
> As at creation when God spoke, and the worlds came into being, so in judgement his voice is an adequate vehicle to

1. Henry, *Commentary to the Whole Bible in One Volume.*
2. Keck, *Interpreter's Bible Commentary.*

> convey the destructive forces focused on the assembled powers of evil.[3]
>
> There is hope in hiding in God. God is our refuge. A refuge is a place where you go that is safe. God is our stronghold. When the enemy is attacking, they can never destroy us. God is our salvation. We were enemies of God because of sin. We are guilty, and we deserve to be destroyed; but through the blood of Jesus Christ we can be saved.[4]

REFLECTIONS

No matter what is happening around us in the world—earthquakes, floods, disease, wars, famine, poverty, and exploitation—God is sovereign. He knows and cares for us in our times of need. Far from having a life of ease and luxury, Jesus warns us that we will experience suffering. But God is our safe hiding place.

3. Bruce, *International Bible Commentary*.

4. https://www.sermoncentral.com/sermons/the-hope-that-comes-from-refuge-shawn-drake-sermon-on-hope-209974?page=2

APPLICATIONS

Amos

My chosen verse ______________________________________

The Context

What commentators say

My reflections

My application

Obadiah

My chosen verse ______________________________

The Context

What commentators say

My reflections

My application

Jonah

My chosen verse ____________________________________

The Context

What commentators say

My reflections

My application

Micah

My chosen verse ____________________________________

The Context

What commentators say

My reflections

My application

NAHUM 3:16

Your merchants have multiplied until they outnumber the stars. But like a swarm of locusts, they strip the land and fly away. NLT

CONTEXT

The pride and self-confidence of the people of Nineveh was futile. Both their merchants and their enemies would strip and plunder them.

COMMENTARY

> The Assyrians' . . . insatiable desire for more, stirred them on to dominate the trade of the world . . . But, although the number of Nineveh's merchants was astronomical, it would do them no good . . . In a day in which 'church growth' has become the passing fad, Nahum's prophecy has something directly to say. The LORD is not impressed by numbers.[1]

REFLECTIONS

Business, commerce, and the market economy have so often been shown for their frailty, short-sightedness, and greed. Often integrity, ethics, morals, and values are sacrificed to the god of

1. Robertson, *Books of Nahum, Habakkuk and Zephaniah.*

self-righteous independence on the altar of nepotism and insatiability. This life on earth is so short, and so insecure, and we cannot take anything with us when we die!

We need to store up for ourselves treasures in heaven.

APPLICATIONS

Habakkuk 3:16

When I heard it, my stomach did flips. I stammered and stuttered. My bones turned to water. I staggered and stumbled. I sit back and wait for Doomsday to descend on our attackers. MSG

CONTEXT

Hope is founded on a holy fear of the LORD.

The One who has joy in store for those who sow in tears also has rest in store for those who tremble in His presence.[1]

COMMENTARY

There is hope in changing from crying to praising. Everyone here today has something that they can cry about. We have pain- Whether it is physical pain, emotional pain, or spiritual pain; we all have pain. You can either cry about it, or you can praise God regardless of the pain. Listed in his song, Habakkuk gives us 3 reasons to praise the LORD.

I will rest in God. Stop spending your time worrying and losing sleep over things that you cannot control. Rest in Christ.

1. Henry, *Commentary to the Whole Bible in One Volume.*

> I will rejoice in God. Have you ever considered where you would be without Jesus Christ? You should be celebrating and rejoicing that you have God in your life.
>
> I will rely on God. Who do you really put your trust in? If it is anyone or anything besides God, it will fail. Do not forget that God is dependable, and you can rely on Him for all things.[2]

REFLECTIONS

Fear, anxiety, and worry are common to all people, to a greater or lesser extent. Personally speaking, I can certainly empathize with the prophet when he said that his stomach did flips. But there is so much about our lives that we fear, and which turns out not to come true. We should listen to Paul when he encourages us to not to be anxious about anything, but instead to pray about everything, and then the LORD will give us His very special peace

2. https://www.sermoncentral.com/sermons/the-hope-that-comes-from-an-attitude-change-shawn-drake-sermon-on-hope-210214?page=2

APPLICATIONS

Zephaniah 3:16

Jerusalem, the time is coming, when it will be said to you: Don't be discouraged or grow weak from fear! CEV

CONTEXT

This prophetic exhortation of salvation demonstrates that after God promises to remove their sin, so then He promises to take away their trouble.

Those who love God with all their heart, need all their heart to rejoice in Him.[1]

COMMENTARY

The expression 'fear not' usually accompanies the assurance of YHWH's presence to save.[2]

The pictures Zephaniah paints for us . . . are awesome. There, in the streets of Jerusalem, are the faithful people of God holding carnival—shouting out their joy to one another, exulting with dance and timbrel and laughter over the fact that God rules their lives . . . It is a celebration that we Christians sometimes have known on Easter morn, when God's trumpets have sounded in

1. Henry, *Commentary to the Whole Bible in One Volume.*
2. Brown, *New Jerome Biblical Commentary.*

> our sanctuaries and in our hearts Hs victory over death and evil.[3]
>
> There is hope in God's strength. With God on your side, you have nothing to fear. There is no reason to fear the enemy when you belong to God. This is not just a mental strength; but a strength that encourages you to action. Through Christ, you can do all things.[4]
>
> The phrase 'On that day' (3:16) is eschatological and points to a future new day for Jerusalem. No longer will Jerusalem and its inhabitants experience the Day of the LORD, a day of wrath (1:2– 2:3). The phrase 'Do not fear, Zion' (3:16) is a typical reassurance formula . . . [Many] verses foreshadow the end of the Babylonian exile and the return of the Judahites to their land.[5]

REFLECTIONS

"Fear not!" usually accompanies God's assurance of salvation. Discouragement and disappointment are known by everyone. But Jesus promises to give us His perfect love, which overcomes all fear.

3. Achtemeier, *Nahum—Malachi.*

4. https://www.sermoncentral.com/sermons/27-27-the-hope-that-comes-from-salvation-shawn-drake-sermon-on-hope-210307?ref=SermonSeriesDetails

5. Brown, *New Jerome Biblical Commentary.*

APPLICATIONS

Haggai

My chosen verse ______________________________

The Context

What commentators say

My reflections

My application

Zechariah

My chosen verse ______________________________

The Context

What commentators say

My reflections

My application

Malachi 3:16

Then those who feared the LORD [with awe-filled reverence] spoke to one another; and the LORD paid attention and heard it, and a book of remembrance was written before Him of those who fear the LORD [with an attitude of reverence and respect] and who esteem His name.
AMP

CONTEXT

The fear of the LORD is the beginning of wisdom. Talking in awe of the LORD echoes the conversation between the two on the road to Emmaus, and so Jesus joined them.

COMMENTARY

> So this group in verse 16 are those who treasure and hold valuable and esteem the kingship of God. Where there treasure is—with God—there is their heart also; and so they 'fear' God, that is, they spend their lives in trust and obedience and reverence and service to God the King. It is the attitude which the LORD will find among all nations when the Kingdom of God comes on earth.[1]
>
> In contrast to the 'arrogant', there is a faithful remnant who truly reverence the LORD, encourage one another through regular fellowship, and meditate often

1. Achtemeier, *Nahum—Malachi.*

> concerning His character. Because they remembered YHWH, He has remembered them.[2]
>
> There is hope in living a life that honors God. Do you ever ask yourself, Why do I bother trying to do the right thing? Why should I try to be without sin when God forgives me of my sin? Let me give you the short answer: It's because God loves you. You are God's treasured possession. Notice that I said possession. If you are a Christian, then God owns you; but instead of treating you as a slave, Jesus treats you as a friend. You should want to please God with the way you do everything.[3]

REFLECTIONS

What a wonderful promise of eternal life—even here in Old Testament! When we put our faith in our LORD and Savior Jesus Christ, He writes our names in two places—in the Lamb's Book of Life, and on the palm of His hand!

2. Bruce, *International Bible Commentary.*

3. https://www.sermoncentral.com/sermons/28-28-the-hope-that-comes-from-being-god-s-treasured-possession-shawn-drake-sermon-on-hope-210623?ref=SermonSeriesDetails

APPLICATIONS

Matthew 3:16

After his baptism, as Jesus came up out of the water, the heavens were opened, and he saw the Spirit of God descending like a dove and settling on him. NLT

CONTEXT

Anointing is central in Jewish thought and life to the public recognition and identification of prophets, priests, and kings. Supremely, Mashiach is the Anointed One. And that is why Peter, Paul and the other apostles declared so frequently that Jesus of Nazareth is the long-awaited Christ, the Messiah and Savior to all.

The Holy Spirit anointed Jesus.

> In Jewish literature, the dove is the symbol of Israel.[1]
>
> The dove is a symbol of peace that the Holy Spirit brings to your life. BiOY

See Ps 2

COMMENTARY

> Jewish monarchs had to be anointed before they could speak or act as royal figures. Accordingly, Jesus' ceremony of anointing is recounted here. First is the ritual of purification (baptism) and then the anointing by God's

1. Peake, *Commentary on the Bible.*

own Spirit . . . Jesus submits to the rite of purification, is publicly anointed by God for the office, and then is publicly proclaimed to be God's royal son.[2]

Baptism is pleasing to God. Jesus had humbled Himself, left Heaven, and became a human. At this point, Jesus was 30 years old, and this is when His ministry began. As Jesus was lifted up out of the water, God the Father let His Son know that He was pleased with His actions. Jesus was living out the plan that was going to bring salvation to the world.[3]

In the Gospel of Matthew, Jesus Christ is presented as the Messiah, the anointed one. He is the true king of Israel. His royal pedigree establishes his claim to the messianic title. The special character of his birth and the pattern of his early life further reinforce this identity: he is conceived by the Holy Spirit and recapitulates Israel's history by sojourning in Egypt. However, it is his baptism that finally realizes the identity and purpose that had been previously intimated. It is the coronation of the true king, the Messiah, the Son of God. Through this baptismal rite, Jesus Christ was formally invested into the high office to which he had been called and for which he had been prepared by God. Kings were merely anointed with oil, but God's Holy Spirit descended upon Jesus, in the form of a dove, and touched him.[4]

REFLECTIONS

Every adult believer who has followed Jesus through the waters of baptism remembers the occasion as if it were yesterday. For me, I came up out of the water and felt as if the angels had scrubbed me clean on the inside!

2. Foster, *Renovaré Spiritual Formation Bible.*

3. https://www.sermoncentral.com/sermons/the-hope-that-comes-from-baptism-shawn-drake-sermon-on-hope-210934?page=2

4. Jarvis and Johnson, *Feasting on the Gospels—Matthew vol.* 1.

APPLICATIONS

Mark 3:16

He appointed his Twelve and gave Simon the nickname Peter the Rock.
TPT

CONTEXT

Simon Peter later made his public declaration that Jesus is the Christ, the Son of the Living God. It is on the bedrock of truth of that public confession of faith that Jesus is able to build His church.

> Naming is more than labelling; the name represents the person as such, so that to bestow a new name represents a change of being and status. Simon is given the name Peter, a Greek word meaning rock. It is not simply a nickname, Rocky, but suggests foundation (Matt 16:18) and pillar (Gal 2:9). Rock also evokes the renaming of Abram as Abraham, who stands at the beginning of God's covenant with Israel as the channel of blessing to all peoples (Gen 12:1– 3; 17:5), and who in this role is called rock (Isa 51:1– 2). Both Jesus and the narrator will always use this new name for Simon throughout the narrative.[5]

5. Boring, *Mark*.

COMMENTARY

These twelve had all kinds of faults, but whatever else could be said of them, they loved Jesus and they were not afraid to tell the world that they loved Him—and that is being a Christian . . . It is significant that Christianity began with a group. The Christian faith is something which from the beginning had to be discovered and lived out in fellowship.[6]

Jesus appointed these 12 men as Apostles. We all know how unlikely candidates they all were to be Apostles; but we are also unlikely candidates to be God's children. Aren't you glad that God doesn't see us like we see one another? We need to see that they were called to be apostles so that He could send them out to preach and they were given the authority to cast out demons.

As Christians, we have been called to tell people about Jesus Christ and have been given the authority to cast out demons, heal the sick, etc . . . Jesus told us that through the power of the Holy Spirit, we can do greater things than He did.[7]

You are accepted. You are accepted, accepted by that which is greater than you, and the name of which you do not know. Do not ask for the name now; perhaps you will find it later. Do not try to do anything now; perhaps later you will do much. Do not seek for anything; do not perform anything; do not intend anything. Simply accept the fact that you are accepted! Paul Tillich.[8]

6. Barclay, *Mark*.

7 https://www.sermoncentral.com/sermons/the-hope-that-comes-from-being-attractive-shawn-drake-sermon-on-hope-210935?page=2

8. http://www.azquotes.com/quote/689736

REFLECTIONS

I have been called out by name. I have been deliberately selected and chosen. Jesus knows me by name. Unlike those awful occasions in childhood when neither side wanted to pick me to be on their team, God carefully and intentionally nominated me and gave me a name before the foundation of all creation.

The meaning of my names David Alan affirms His calling on my life: 'Beloved and Precious'.

APPLICATIONS

Luke 3:16

John answered them all by saying, As for me, I baptize you [only] with water; but One who is mightier [more powerful, more noble] than I is coming, and I am not fit to untie the strap of His sandals [even as His slave]. He will baptize you [who truly repent] with the Holy Spirit and [you who remain unrepentant] with fire. AMP

CONTEXT

Jesus' baptism imparts greater power than John's.

The Aramaic implies that they would be the ones who would do the baptizing:

John baptized you in water, but you will baptize [others] in the Holy Spirit. Acts 1:5 TPT

> Then God will purge by His truth all the deeds of man, refining for Himself some of mankind in order to remove every evil spirit from the midst of their flesh, to cleanse them with the Holy Spirit from all wicked practices and sprinkle them with a spirit of truth like purifying water.[1]

COMMENTARY

> John's humility gives a proper perspective on the relationship of humanity to Jesus. Human beings are

1. https://www.essene.com/History&Essenes/md.htm

> not Jesus' advisers or equals; they are greatly honoured to know Him and serve Him . . . Jesus baptizes with the Spirit, bringing blessing, discernment, enablement and divine presence.[2]

> The incarnation, preaching, and death of Jesus Christ were designed to represent, proclaim, and purchase for us this gift of the Spirit Wesley.[3]

> The Holy Spirit streams into the heart and makes a new man, one who now loves God and gladly does his will. Such is the Holy Spirit himself, or rather the work he does in the heart. He writes in fiery flame on the heart and makes it alive, causing it to find expression in fiery tongue and active hand; a new man is made, who is conscious of a reason, heart, and mind unlike he formerly had. Everything is now alive: He has a live reason; he has light and courage and a heart which burns with love and delights in whatever pleases God. This is the real difference between the written and the spiritual laws of God; and such is the work of the Holy Spirit. Luther.[4]

REFLECTIONS

I was baptized in the Holy Spirit at the same time that I gave my heart and life to the LORD. He welcomed me into His family. Since that time, the Holy Spirit has continually brought me closer to Jesus. He causes God's fruit to grow in me. He donates His special gifts to me to serve Him. And He allows me to experience His wrap-around love.

2. Bock, *Luke*.

3. http://wesley.nnu.edu/john-wesley/the-sermons-of-john-wesley-1872-edition/sermon-141-on-the-holy-spirit/

4. http://lenker.webdesign-ontario.com/[17]Pentecost_percent20Johnpercent2014-23-31.pdf

APPLICATIONS

So, here we are! This is what started me on this wonderful adventure of sharing these thoughts with you!

JOHN 3:16

Indeed, in just the same way, God the Father acted in love on another occasion, this time for the whole rebellious human race, by sacrificing his only natural Son so that all who go on trusting and obeying him might never be ruined beyond recovery, but go on having everlasting and abundant life. [1]

CONTEXT

This is my own personal testimony:

> Long my imprisoned spirit lay
> Fast bound in sin and nature's night;
> Thine eye diffused a quick'ning ray,
> I woke, the dungeon flamed with light;
> My chains fell off, my heart was free;
> I rose, went forth and followed Thee. Wesley

> The Incarnation and Crucifixion . . . are a demonstration in action of the love of God, which is their cause and motive.[2]

> There is a God, and His love is wide enough to embrace all humankind without distinction or exception. It is not a vague or sentimental love. God's love is of immeasurable intensity, demonstrated by His willingness to sacrifice His only Son for you and me. BiOY

1. Pawson, *Is John 3:16 the Gospel?*
2. Peake, *Commentary on the Bible.*

COMMENTARY

The work of Christ finds its origin in the Father's love; this is the only 'reason' behind His self-revelation. Love is not merely a continuous attitude of God. He has acted. In Christ He gave His unique Son, the very image of Himself. His love is reciprocal. Only those may enjoy it who respond by receiving God's gift in Christ. And when they receive Him, their response is inevitably one of giving back their love to God.[3]

Having 'eternal life' is in the present tense. Too often we imagine eternal life only in the future. How does it change our discipleship if we live eternal life now?[4]

The new birth isn't merely a psychological or emotional experience. It isn't turning over a new leaf. It doesn't come about by simply going to church, or being baptized, or confirmed. It is something far more radical.[5]

The whole substance of our salvation is not to be sought anywhere else than in Christ . . . He ascribes the glory for our salvation entirely to His love . . . Therefore it is mercy alone reconciles us to God and at the same time restores us to life. Calvin.[6]

God said, 'Because my son Jesus Christ has taken the death and the hell and the judgement that you deserved, if you will believe on him, if you will trust in him, if you will commit your life to him, I will forgive you, I will bury your sins in the depths of the sea, I will save you. I will take you to heaven.' Billy Graham.[7]

3. Bruce, *International Bible Commentary.*
4. Foster, *Renovaré Spiritual Formation Bible.*
5. *Listening to God—Eight weeks with John.*
6. Calvin, *The Gospel According to St. John.*
7. Graham, 20 *Centuries of Great Preaching vol. XII*

He gave His Son to make atonement due to law, then gave and sent His Holy Spirit to take charge of this work. Finney.[8]

God loves the unlovable world as much as He loves the Son . . . His divine love flows even to those who do not deserve it.[9]

Before we can begin to see the cross as something done for us, we have to see it as something done by us.[10]

Many Christians, whether Catholic or Protestant, liberal or conservative, have imagined a story like this. (1) We messed up badly; (2) God had to punish us; (3) fortunately, his innocent son got in the way and took the rap. But the Bible tells a bigger, more subtle story.

Paul's summary of the Christian message begins, 'The Messiah died for our sins in accordance with the scriptures'. That doesn't mean in accordance with the story we have in our heads, with a few biblical footnotes. Paul is referring to the entire story of Israel's ancient scriptures.

That story is not about 'sin and what God does with it.' It's about creation and covenant. N.T. Wright.[11]

There is tremendous relief in knowing that His love to me is based at every point on prior knowledge of the worst about me. J.I. Packer.[12]

To be a Christian means to forgive the inexcusable because God has forgiven the inexcusable in you. CS Lewis.[13]

8. Finney, 20 *Centuries of Great Preaching vol. XII*

9. Kanagaraj, *Gospel of John.*

10. Stott, *The Cross.*

11. http://www.foxnews.com/opinion/2017/02/16/n-t-wright-why-cross-matters-more-than-think.html

12. Packer, *In God's Presence: Daily Devotions.*

13. Lewis, *'On Forgiveness'.*

> Let's not forget the significance of that little word "only". In that word, we see something of the depths of the Father's love for the world and the price he was willing to pay for the salvation of his people. Karl Barth.[14]

> Here we have the very heart and essence of the whole Gospel, that Jesus Christ came to seek and to save people from death and restore them to life. Matthew Henry.[15]

> It is a distinctively Christian idea that God's love is wide enough to embrace all mankind. His love is not confined to any national group or any spiritual elite. It is a love which proceeds from the fact that He is love. F.F. Bruce.[16]

> These words, pronounced by Jesus during the conversation with Nicodemus, summarize a theme that is at the center of the Christian proclamation: even when a situation seems desperate, God intervenes, offering man salvation and joy. God, in fact, doesn't stand apart, but enters into the history of humanity, He 'involves' Himself in our life; He enters it, to animate it with His grace and to save it. Pope Francis.[17]

REFLECTIONS

I am rather nervous about adding anything to the comments above by all these renowned writers and speakers.

However, I can say that I am utterly convinced—beyond any doubt whatsoever—that, even if I had been the only person on earth, Jesus would still have come and died for me.

14. http://www.rcnzonline.com/fnf/a88.htm
15. Henry, *Commentary to the Whole Bible in One Volume.*
16. Bruce, *International Bible Commentary.*
17. Pope Francis, *Angelus Address.*

APPLICATIONS

Acts 3:16

And because of the trustworthiness of His name, His name healed him whom you now see and know, and the faith, that which is through Him, has given him wholeness in the presence of all of you. [1]

CONTEXT

While Jesus was alive here on Earth, faith was placed in Him as a person; now, it is placed firmly in His name, His continuing, and present power.

Our preaching should always be Jesus-centered. BiOY

COMMENTARY

The name of Jesus is not a talisman, or a good luck charm. The Name is not to be treated lightly. It must be remembered that this Name packs behind it all the authority in heaven and in earth and earth may be limited but heaven is unlimited![2]

The Name, that is, the whole Christ, in His nature, His offices, His work, His Incarnation, His Life, His Death, Resurrection, Sitting at the right hand of God—it is

1. Witherington, *Acts of the Apostles.*

2. https://www.sermoncentral.com/sermons/his-name-through-faith-in-his-name-victor-ramlall-sermon-on-apostles-peter-158578?ref=SermonSerps

> this Christ whose Name made that man strong and will make us strong. Brethren, let us remember that, while fragments of the Name will have fragmentary power, as the curative virtue that resides in any substance belongs to the smallest grain of it, if detached from the mass—whilst fragments of the Name of Christ have power, thanks be to Him! so that no man can have even a very imperfect and rudimentary view of what Jesus Christ is and does, without getting strength and healing in proportion to the completeness of his conception, yet in order to realize all that He can be and do, a man must take the whole Christ as He is revealed.[3]

REFLECTIONS

I still wince whenever somebody uses the name of my God, or my Jesus, as a swear word. How much more must it hurt Him. If only everyone was aware of the love, the power, and the riches contained in His name.

Indeed, I have on my shelf a book listing and exploring the hundreds of names of God.

3. Maclaren, *Expositions of Holy Scriptures: Acts.*

Acts 3:16

APPLICATIONS

Romans 3:16

Wherever they go, they destroy and make people suffer NLT

CONTEXT

> We long for peace. We long to be in a right relationship with God and with other people. BiOY

Quoted from Isa 59:7-8—a lament for Israel's sins—Paul is here emphasizing the hopelessness of our search for peace without the Prince of Peace.

And Rom 1:29-32 shows clearly the extent of evil in our lives and the world.

COMMENTARY

> Cursing and bitterness are there in all of us, and we have all been guilty of them. You have simply to listen to the things people say when they are off guard, and to what they say about one another. Martyn Lloyd Jones. [1]

> Paul believed men without Christ to be bad, but he never believed them to be too bad to be saved. He was confident that what Christ had done for him, Christ could do for any man. William Barclay. [2]

1. Lloyd Jones, *Romans—Exposition of* 2:1—3:20.
2. Barclay, *Romans.*

> This expression which Paul adds from Isaiah, destruction and misery are in their ways, is a most striking one, for it is a description of ferocity of immeasurable barbarity, which produces solitude and waste, by destroying everything wherever it goes. Pliny gives this same description of Domitian. Calvin.[3]

REFLECTIONS

We are all very aware of our sins, weaknesses, and mistakes. Our rebellion against the will of God comes easily to mind. That is because we are so often faced with God's holiness. The good news is that Jesus has rescued us from all our sins and all our diseases.

3. https://ccel.org/ccel/calvin/calcom38/calcom38.vii.v.html

APPLICATIONS

1 Corinthians 3:16

Do you not discern and understand that you [the whole church at Corinth] are God's temple (His sanctuary), and that God's Spirit has His permanent dwelling in you [to be at home in you, collectively as a church and also individually]? AMP

CONTEXT

God is concerned that we don't just belong to Him, but instead that we are the very place where He dwells

In this passage we have clear evidence for affirming the divinity of the Holy Spirit. Calvin.[1]

COMMENTARY

Based on everything Paul has already said, he adds to our understanding that not only are we the holiest of holies for God, but that His Spirit actually lives inside us. This is the most important part of Acts 3:16. This means God accompanies us wherever we go. This means God is inside us living in us as our constant companion. He is our Counselor. This is not the way the Holy Spirit worked in the past. The Holy Spirit was given and then taken away. The Holy Spirit was given to select people and not to most others. By the time Jesus was born and

1. https://www.studylight.org/commentary/1-corinthians/3-16.html

lived, the Jewish people had put God in a box. They thought their God lived in a certain land in a certain city and in a certain room in the Temple. This simply isn't true. In fact, Stephen says in Acts 7, The God who made the world and everything in it is the LORD of heaven and earth and does not live in temples built by hands. 25 And he is not served by human hands, as if he needed anything, because he himself gives all men life and breath and everything else (verses 24-25). God is not and cannot be localized into one spot.[2]

The temple in the Old Testament can be seen as 'a type' of the temple in the New Testament (the people of God). In this passage, we have a description of the temple, which Solomon spent seven years building (1 Kgs 6:38). It was designed to be the dwelling place for the presence of God on earth: 'I'll personally take up my residence' (v.13, MSG) . . . The temple in the Old Testament points forward to the people of God. We are God's house. God lives in us individually. Your body is the temple of the Holy Spirit (1 Cor 6:19). The church today is the holy temple of the LORD in which God lives by his Spirit (Eph 2:21–22). This is God's 'house' today. BiOY

REFLECTIONS

I find it completely amazing that God lives in me!

2. https://www.sermoncentral.com/sermons/temple-is-as-temple-does-troy-borst-sermon-on-body-as-a-temple-196560?page=3

APPLICATIONS

2 Corinthians 3:16

But the moment one turns to the LORD with an open heart, the veil is lifted, and they see. TPT

CONTEXT

> You may see a thousand faces a day, images are everywhere, but the Spirit reveals the most important face of all to us. As you spend time in the presence of the LORD you become more and more like Him. You are transformed into His likeness with ever-increasing glory. BiOY

See Heb:20
This is Paul's own testimony—Gal.1:16

COMMENTARY

> There is only one way to uplift or remove the veil. You must believe in Jesus Christ. It is only by turning in faith to Christ that the veil over the reading of Moses or God's Word is removed. The shining of the moon can be understood only in terms of the shining of the sun of which it is a less glorious reflection. It is one and the same light.[1]

1. https://www.sermoncentral.com/sermons/the-reflection-of-his-glory-dennis-davidson-sermon-on-transformation-187538?page=3

Christ removes the veil, giving eternal life and freedom from trying to be saved by keeping laws. And without the veil, we can be like mirrors reflecting God's glory.[2]

The LORD is the Spirit, and where He is there is liberty from the law.[3]

REFLECTIONS

At the very moment of Christ's crucifixion, God caused the ripping of the veil from top to bottom. It was 20 feet wide, 60 feet high, and 4 inches thick! Finally, we have access to the most holy place, which is the very presence of God.

2. *Life Application Study Bible.*
3. Peake, *Commentary on the Bible.*

APPLICATIONS

GALATIANS 3:16

Remember the royal proclamation God spoke over Abraham and to Abraham's child? God said that his promises were made to pass on to Abraham's Child, not children. And who is this Child? It is the Son of promise, Jesus, the anointed Messiah! TPT

CONTEXT

> God's promise was originally given to Abraham and his seed. Paul explains that Jesus is God's promise. BiOY

This is echoed in 2 Sam 7:12-14

> Both eternal life and perishing, being end-time events, are opposed to each other. The former denotes salvation of the believers and the latter the eternal condemnation of those who do not believe in the Son. Human destiny has only these two ends. Such dualism is used in John to urge human beings to choose life.[1]

COMMENTARY

> God's promise was given long before the Mosaic law appeared . . . it was given . . . to Christ . . . and Christ's own.[2]

1. Kanagaraj, *Gospel of John.*
2. Longenecker, *Galatians.*

> The covenant that God made with Abraham was not to ever be broken, only fulfilled. Nothing or no one could change the promises given to Abraham by the Heavenly Father. The Law could not change the promise! No Jew or Gentile could change the promise! No Judaizer could change the promise! Not even God's covenant with Moses changed God's promises to Abraham. Simply stated. God's promises will endure! I have no doubt that there are some here today who are trusting in the wrong things to get you to Heaven. No matter what you believe No matter what you have been taught; regardless of any traditions, rules, or rituals that you observe, if you die without a personal relationship with Jesus, a lake of fire will be your final destination!
>
> But God has made a promise that if you will put your faith, hope, and trust in His only begotten Son: You can be delivered! You can be redeemed! You can be freed from the chains of sin that you are bound in today!
>
> I beg you to make the choice today to trust in God's Enduring Promise. [3]

> The Jews were never able to live up to [the law]. By making sinners of them all, it deprived them of any claim to the fulfilment of the promise made to Abraham. As sinners, they could receive the inheritance only as a pure gift. Christ, whose death brings the interim period of the law to an end, is now offering them the inheritance, along with forgiveness of their sins, as a free gift, if they will believe.[4]

REFLECTIONS

All of God's promises are true, and are still as relevant today. We can stand firm on the promises of God.

3. https://www.sermoncentral.com/sermons/god-s-enduring-promise-part-1-kevin-l-jones-sermon-on-god-s-promises-188145?page=5

4. Bligh, *Galatians*.

APPLICATIONS

Ephesians 3:16

And I pray that he would unveil within you the unlimited riches of his glory and favor until supernatural strength floods your innermost being with his divine might and explosive power. TPT

CONTEXT

God's power is revealed . . . the power of the gospel; the power of unity; the power of the Holy Spirit. BiOY

The flow of his prayer is that God would grant them strength through his Spirit and that Christ would dwell in them, and that the Ephesians would be strong both in understanding and in knowing, which can be summed up as being filled with or into God's fullness.[1]

COMMENTARY

It is the Spirit who will strengthen them in their inner being. They need this power and strengthening to face this world in which they have to stand for Christ, a world in which they sometimes feel powerless and alone.[2]

The reason why some of us struggle so much with sin is that we are relying on our own power to deal with it. We

1. Cohick, *A New Covenant Commentary.*
2. Gardner, *Ephesians.*

> think that if we think it through on our own we will figure out a solution. Some of us struggle with relationships because we rely on our own power to deal with it.[3]

> The power of God which is effective in humanity is the Holy Spirit, which is mediated through the spiritual word of preaching . . . and baptism . . . and lives on in Christians as the 'Spirit of faith' . . . and binds them to Christ and makes them steadfast.[4]

> Strength through the power of the Spirit is a distinctive and recurring theme . . . Paul understands the 'inner person' . . . of the believer in Christ turned towards and waiting expectantly for the life of the age to come, delighting in God's law . . . being renewed daily . . . and here being strengthened by the Holy Spirit.[5]

REFLECTIONS

Paul sometimes gets carried away, heaping up ever-increasing exaltations to God in his love for Him. Perhaps we too should more often become overwhelmed by Jesus and be lost in His wonder, love, and praise.

It is in and through the Holy Spirit that we are able to speak truth to power.

3. https://www.sermoncentral.com/sermons/family-prayer-freddy-fritz-sermon-on-love-227786?page=2

4. https://www.sermoncentral.com/sermons/god-s-enduring-promise-part-1-kevin-l-jones-sermon-on-god-s-promises-188145?page=5

5. Muddiman. Epistle to the Ephesians.

APPLICATIONS

PHILIPPIANS 3:16

Only let's be sure to keep in line with the position we have reached. BfE

CONTEXT

We need increasingly to see our lives from God's perspective.

> The thing in which all Christians agree is that they must make Christ all in all and set their hearts on another world.[1]

COMMENTARY

> We must take advantage of every opportunity, of everyday, of every moment to live life on purpose!! Unfortunately, however, many times we get so caught up in the details of our day to day life that we just don't take the time to seize every moment![2]

> Gregory of Nyssa saw the totality of the spiritual life as an '*epektasis*,' a continual growth or straining ahead, as in the words of St. Paul, 'Forgetting the past, I strain for what is still to come.'[3]

1. Henry, *Commentary to the Whole Bible in One Volume.*

2. https://www.sermoncentral.com/sermons/live-like-you-were-dying-ben-johnson-sermon-on-finding-fulfillment-102290?ref=SermonSerps

3. Fowl, *Philippians.*

> If it be once admitted that our perfection after all amounts only to relative stages of imperfection, we shall realize more clearly that we are all working toward the same goal, and shall be ready to help one another instead of criticizing or envying one another.[4]

REFLECTIONS

Let the main thing be the main thing. It's all about having Jesus as my focus, imagining Him beckoning towards me, just beyond the finishing line. He desires to be my goal, my purpose, my ambition.

4. Beare, *Philippians*.

APPLICATIONS

Colossians 3:16

Let the word [spoken by] Christ (the Messiah) have its home [in your hearts and minds] and dwell in you in [all its] richness, as you teach and admonish and train one another in all insight and intelligence and wisdom [in spiritual things, and as you sing] psalms and hymns and spiritual songs, making melody to God with [His] grace in your hearts. AMP

CONTEXT

The word of Christ is not found elsewhere in Paul's writing; the 'logos' is seen as the divine essence throughout the universe and present in each individual soul.

And your hearts will overflow with a joyful song to the LORD YHWH. Keep speaking to each other with words of Scripture, singing the Psalms with praises and spontaneous songs given by the Spirit! Eph 5:19 TPT

Teaching and preaching must come out of a life in which the words of Christ live in the heart.

COMMENTARY

> Only the truth can set us free. Only the truth can satisfy our soul. Only the truth can make us care for others. Only the truth can make us grow spiritually. So, to become a change-agent, we must first experience change

through the Word. The word dwell means, to be at home. We are to make sure that the word of God would take permanent residence in our lives.

Importantly, the mechanism by which this word of Messiah is communicated is through instruction (teaching and admonishing each other) and in worship (singing psalms, hymns, and spiritual songs), 42 and all of this is to occur in The Context of thanksgiving . 43 If we regard the impartation of the word of Messiah as the goal of teaching, admonishing, and singing, then we are led to the conclusion that teaching is meant to take on a worshipful character while musical praise is to take on a didactic role in order to comprehensively impart the word. Christian teaching is not meant to be dry, but soaked in thankful praise. Similarly, singing is not purposed to be doctrinally benign but should comprise a pointer to the truth of Jesus Christ.[1]

REFLECTIONS

I love to study the Word of God, and to meditate on it.

That has been the motivation for this book. The Bible has the power to change lives. As I spend time receiving all that He has for me in the scriptures, so He enables me to become more like His Son.

1. Bird, *Colossians and Philemon.*

APPLICATIONS

1 Thessalonians

My chosen verse ______________________________

The Context

What commentators say

My reflections

My application

2 Thessalonians 3:16

Now, may the LORD himself, the LORD of peace, pour into you his peace in every circumstance and in every possible way. The LORD's tangible presence be with you all. TPT

CONTEXT

The LORD of Peace is one of the names of God—Judg 6:24

In Greek, 'peace' is *eirene*, which is the root of the word 'serene'. Peace is the tranquil state of a soul assured of its salvation through Christ, and so fearing nothing from God and content with its earthly lot, the blessed state of devout and upright people after death.

COMMENTARY

> Jesus is the LORD of peace because He is the only one who can bring peace. The phrase himself is emphatic, meaning that it is Jesus, and only Jesus who can give us peace.[1]

> *Shalom* is used in the Old Testament to bid welfare or express harmony and concord among people. It is also used to indicate the wellness, material prosperity, physical safety, and peace of a person, a city, a country, or

1. https://www.sermoncentral.com/sermons/being-busy-for-christ-brian-bill-sermon-on-second-coming-56231?page=7

> between two entities that relate to each other. It mainly denotes health, inner peace, and spiritual well-being. It is always found in association with righteousness and truth, but not with wickedness.
>
> The original source of all shalom is God. When he harnessed chaos into order in creation, he bestowed shalom for the whole of it. In fact, he claims, I make [shalom] (Isa 45:7). Therefore, John Goldingay concludes:
>
> God is the maker of shalom . . . [that] stands potentially for all forms of well-being. It covers peace, but it is another positive term that embraces much more than the absence of conflict; it suggests a community enjoying fullness of life, prosperity, contentment, harmony, and happiness. Its antonym is *ra*, an all-purpose word for what is bad, both covering evil and adversity.[2]

REFLECTIONS

On occasions, I like to plan and prepare, to manage and organise. However, when circumstances change beyond my control, I quickly lose my peace. It is then that my caring LORD smiles and beckons me towards Him again, wrapping His arms of love round me, reminding me that it is He who is totally sovereign. And then once more His peace returns.

2. http://www.lausanneworldpulse.com/themedarticles-php/1089/02-2009

APPLICATIONS

1 TIMOTHY 3:16

Indeed the mystery of godliness is certainly great:
he was revealed in the flesh,
and vindicated in the spirit;
he appeared to angels,
and was announced to Gentiles;
he was believed in the world,
and taken up in glory. BfE

CONTEXT

This verse is a confession of faith or a fragment from an early hymn. It can be seen as the gospel in a nutshell.

> Viewed entirely, the hymn arches from Bethlehem to the heights of heavenly majesty; the Savior is seen as the object of angelic contemplation and the subject of apostolic preaching: and He is acclaimed as the One vindicated not only in His Spirit, but also in the hearts of all who believe in Him. F.F. Bruce.[1]

The historic creeds proclaim, in different ways, Christ's:

Incarnation, resurrection, and ascension, followed by His preaching, belief, and glorification.

1. Bruce, *International Bible Commentary.*

COMMENTARY

Christianity is a mystery . . . It is Christ; He is God revealed in the flesh; He is justified in the Spirit; He was seen by angels; He is preached to the gentiles; He was believed by the world; He was received up into glory.[2]

Paul gives us a concise vision of the mystery, in the form of a hymn: three sets of pairs each having a heavenly and earthly side to them:

1. Christ's Presentation: God was manifest in the flesh, justified in the Spirit

    a. Here we have the incarnation—manifest in the flesh—earthly

    b. And the resurrection—Proving he was who He said He was the Son of God—heavenly

    c. Both man and God

2. Christ's Witness: seen of angels, preached unto the Gentiles

    a. Christ was seen of angels, the heavenly: angels were at his birth, his trial in the desert, the garden, and the resurrection

    b. The earthly, He was preached to the Gentiles—both Jew and Gentile heard of him through the apostles to be both LORD and Savior.

3. Christ's Reception, believed on in the world, received up into glory.

    a. The earthly, men received Him as LORD and Savior

2. Henry, *Commentary to the Whole Bible in One Volume.*

b. The heavenly, Jesus was received up into glory, back to His throne in heaven.

C. These are the truths the church is in possession of.

1. We hold them as eternal truths to be to be treasured and testified to.
2. You must believe these eternal truths as a part of God's church.
3. It is our confession as the House of God.[3]

The Christian faith is guaranteed by its inspired scriptures. Once written down, these become for all time the standard for teaching, for reproof, for correction, and for training in righteousness.[4]

REFLECTIONS

We are encouraged to be ready at all times to share the Gospel, whenever the opportunity arises. As with our testimony, we need to have available, at a moment's notice, three forms of the good news: the 'elevator pitch' (30 seconds); the brief summary (3 minutes); and the extended exploration (30 minutes).

3. https://www.sermoncentral.com/sermons/the-house-of-god-duane-smith-sermon-on-church-general-156087?page=4

4. Keck, *Interpreter's Bible Commentary.*

APPLICATIONS

2 Timothy 3:16

Every Scripture is God-breathed (given by His inspiration) and profitable for instruction, for reproof and conviction of sin, for correction of error and discipline in obedience, [and] for training in righteousness (in holy living, in conformity to God's will in thought, purpose, and action) AMP

CONTEXT

The Bible is our authority in all matters of faith and life. BiOY

The scriptures are 'God-breathed', and this description occurs only here. They are divinely breathed-in, and are His Holy in-spiration.

What equips believers in this world is Scripture.[1]

COMMENTARY

The Bible is a gift from God, God speaks to us and other believers around the world today through the pages of the Bible. We need to do more with our Bible than leave it to gather dust on a shelf somewhere at home. We need to read it, study it, believe it.

When we read the Bible, we need to listen to God's word, allow it to penetrate our hearts and minds, allow

1. Henry, *Commentary to the Whole Bible in One Volume.*

it to change and transform us. There is so much we can learn from the Word of God, but it's more than just learning head knowledge. As disciples of Christ, the principles and precepts of God revealed in the Bible need to be learned, applied, and obeyed in our daily lives. Obedience to the word and commands of God. Great in principle, harder in practice.

Our worldview or opinions may be contrary to what God has said—but God is the one who is perfect. We are imperfect and just because we don't agree with God on something it does not make us right and God wrong. If we truly want to be guided by God then even though it may at times be hard, we must be obedient to His word and calling on our lives.

You know that our lives here are brief, when physical death comes, and we leave this world behind, we will awake in eternity. There is more to experience beyond this life—either an eternity with our LORD and Savior in Heaven or eternally separated from God in Hell.

God in His love allows us the choice of where we will spend eternity. If we accept Jesus as LORD and Savior we are assured of a place in Heaven. If we reject God and His free gift of salvation, then by our own free will we are choosing an eternity without God in Hell.

It's either one or the other there is no other option. A simple Yes or No—Accept or Reject choice that seals our final destination. Simply put, God has given us His Word to guide us to our eternal home.[2]

REFLECTIONS

I really love the Bible; but will I allow it to love me?

Jesus is the living Word of God. As I give myself time to immerse myself in Him, I need to be open to Him, and give Him time

2. https://www.sermoncentral.com/sermons/the-bible-is-our-guide-in-this-sin-sick-world-dean-courtier-sermon-on-god-s-word-197203?ref=SermonSerps

to instruct me, reprove me, convict me of sin, correct my errors, discipline me to obey, and to train me in righteous living.

APPLICATIONS

Titus

My chosen verse ________________________________

The Context

What commentators say

My reflections

My application

Philemon

My chosen verse ______________________________

The Context

What commentators say

My reflections

My application

Hebrews 3:16

For who were the people who turned a deaf ear? Weren't they the very ones Moses led out of Egypt? MSG

CONTEXT

The author of Hebrews has just repeated a line from Psalm 95:8 for us. That passage refers to some people who caused God to become angry. The author has a question for his readers. He asks who these people were. Who would actually do such a terrible thing?

Both Matthew 13, the parable of the sower, and Luke 6, the parable of the two houses, emphasize the importance of doing the will of God.

The author insists that, if we desire to bring our pilgrimage to that great rewarding conclusion which God has prepared for Christians, we must make glad and obedient response to His word. We are required to hear, believe, obey and share the word of God.[1]

COMMENTARY

It isn't enough to make a good beginning. As a nation, Israel made a good beginning. After all, it took a lot of faith to cross the Red Sea. Yet all of that first generation perished in the wilderness, except for the two men of

1. Brown, *Message of Hebrews.*

faith—Joshua and Caleb. So, we see that they could not enter in because of unbelief.

In a New Testament context, our belief centers on the superiority of Jesus Christ, the truth of who He is (fully God and fully man) and His atoning work for us as a faithful High Priest . . . When we trust in these things, making them the food of our souls, we enter into God's rest.

If we enter into God's rest, then the coming years will only increase our trust and reliance on Jesus. If by unbelief we fail to enter in, then the coming years will only gradually draw us away from a passionate, trusting relationship with Jesus. [2]

But who was it who caused God to become angry? That is the most terrible fact. It was the people whom God saved. God himself had sent his servant Moses to rescue them from Egypt. God had done wonderful things to make them free. But they were not grateful. They did not obey him with glad hearts. They refused to obey him. They did not want him to have any part of their lives. They even wanted to return to Egypt.

And the shock is this. Today, Christians are the people whom God has saved. And we too can make God angry if we have those same wrong attitudes.[3]

REFLECTIONS

I make God angry.
That is awful—awe-ful.
I know He loves me, but I really don't want to experience His anger.

2. Guzik, *Hebrews*.

3. http://www.usefulbible.com/hebrews/who-makes-god-angry.htm

APPLICATIONS

James 3:16

So, wherever jealousy and selfishness are uncovered, you will also find many troubles and every kind of meanness. TPT

CONTEXT

One sin leads to another, and it cannot be imagined how much trouble is produced.[1]

Speak words of life. Your words have tremendous power for connection. You can bring healing, encouragement, and edification. Your words can change a person's day or even their life. BiOY

COMMENTARY

James advises about how to discern between so-called wisdoms. There is an earthly wisdom that is 'unspiritual, devilish' and leads to 'disorder and wickedness'.[2]

This human wisdom is proud and jealous. It is the cause of disagreement and not peace. Where this wisdom is, there will be confusion. The ambition of man tends to destroy life with God. The works of this wisdom are bad and of no worth. No real benefit for the church can come

1. Henry, *Commentary to the Whole Bible in One Volume.*
2. Foster, *Renovaré Spiritual Formation Bible.*

> from them. They do nothing to help Christians and build the church. These works just destroy the unity that ought to be there.[3]

REFLECTIONS

Jealousy is essentially all about pride. It is selfish and egotistical. When I am jealous, I assume that I am more important than others. Jealousy lacks love, care, and compassion. If I am tempted in this area, I need to confront it with the opposite spirit: to be joyful with others in their success; to enjoy their achievements; to rejoice in their acclaim.

3. https://www.easyenglish.bible/bible-commentary/james-lbw.htm

APPLICATIONS

1 Peter 3:16

Maintain a clean conscience, so that those who slander you for living a pure life in Christ will have to lie about you and will be ashamed because of their slander. TPT

CONTEXT

> Arrogance and rudeness will seldom win people over. As well a verbal defense, you need a moral defense—a clear conscience. BiOY

The phrase 'in Christ' is borrowed directly from Paul (who uses it over 160 times), and before him it was an unknown phrase.

COMMENTARY

> Bold words will not honour the LORD if they are not supported by a consistent life . . . The presence of the Holy Spirit in the heart of the believer brings his conscience before God, with radical results.[1]
>
> 'Conscience' denotes an attitude towards God from which a true attitude toward man will emerge. When the Christian is united to Christ in fellowship on the basis of what God has done for him in the death and resurrection

1. Clowney, *Message of* 1 *Peter.*

> of Christ then his 'behaviour' is 'good' and will be his defense against his accusers.[2]

> Jesus was able to be silent before His accusers because He had nothing on His conscience.[3]

> A 'good conscience' is characteristic of the baptized man who lives in the Spirit.[4]

REFLECTIONS

On management development courses, I often used to encourage the participants to watch my feet, not my lips. Integrity is everything, and essential for good leadership.

2. Best, 1 *Peter.*
3. Leaney, *Letters of Peter and Jude.*
4. Kelly, *Epistles of Peter and Jude.*

APPLICATIONS

2 Peter 3:16

Our good brother Paul, who was given much wisdom in these matters, refers to this in all his letters, and has written you essentially the same thing. Some things Paul writes are difficult to understand. Irresponsible people who don't know what they are talking about twist them every which way. They do it to the rest of the Scriptures, too, destroying themselves as they do it. MSG

CONTEXT

So, by the time Peter wrote this letter, Paul's letters were already regarded as Scripture.

It's important to use scripture to interpret and understand scripture. It's also important to have more than a superficial understanding of scripture, otherwise people can be misled. 'Twisting' God's word is so often a device or strategy of the enemy.

COMMENTARY

It's good to know that those of us who find some of Paul's teaching difficult, are in good company!

> Peter proceeds to tell us that Paul's letters contain some things that are hard to understand . . . because of their obscurity . . . their excellent sublimity . . . and because of the weakness of the human mind.[1]

1. Henry, *Commentary to the Whole Bible in One Volume.*

REFLECTIONS

If we find it difficult to understand some of Paul's teaching, then we're in good company!

So . . . we need to take time, and to reflect, and to . . . .. meditate!

APPLICATIONS

1 John 3:16

This is how we have discovered love's reality: Jesus sacrificed his life for us. Because of this great love, we should be willing to lay down our lives for one another. TPT

CONTEXT

This is Jesus' response to our sin, and our response to His sacrifice. My salvation cost Him His life. The only thing I could add to His sacrifice was my sin. So now He wants me to freely spend my life in sacrificial service to Him.

> Love is not just a feeling. It involves action. BiOY
>
> The second John three sixteen:
> Love so amazing, so divine,
> Demands my soul, my life, my all. F.F. Bruce. [1]
>
> The record of the LORD Jesus Christ is the record of God's love for us.[2]

1. Bruce, *International Bible Commentary.*
2. Henry, *Commentary to the Whole Bible in One Volume.*

COMMENTARY

> Think of the sheer sacrifice of the cross. Jesus laid down His life, quite literally, foregoing the privilege of further time in this world . . . He humbled Himself! He laid aside the visible glory which He had in heaven. Think of the shame, the insult of the cross. Think of the physical side of it . . . John calls us to be like Jesus! The cross is a pattern for us . . . To think that God expects me to be like Jesus![3]

> Having shown that love is the evidence of life, he explains that the essence of love is self-sacrifice, which has been perfectly manifested in Christ.[4]

> The love of Jesus—that is, the loyalty and devotion to His friends, the magnanimity towards His enemies, and the goodwill towards all men, in which He died—is indistinguishably one with the love of the eternal God towards His creatures, which is their only hope and assurance of eternal life.[5]

REFLECTIONS

Jesus denied Himself, gave Himself, and surrendered Himself—for me. He now requires that I deny myself, give myself, and surrender myself—for Him.

Salvation was in God's mind from the beginning. Love is my daily response. That's why He asked Peter—and why He asks us—'Do you love me?'

3. Eaton, 1, 2, *and* 3 *John*.
4. Stott, *Letters of John*.
5. Dodd, *Johannine Epistles*.

APPLICATIONS

2 JOHN

My chosen verse ________________________________

The Context

What commentators say

My reflections

My application

3 John

My chosen verse ________________________________

The Context

What commentators say

My reflections

My application

Jude

My chosen verse ______________________________

The Context

What commentators say

My reflections

My application

Revelation 3:16

I know you inside and out, and find little to my liking. You're not cold, you're not hot—far better to be either cold or hot! You're stale. You're stagnant. You make me want to vomit. MSG

CONTEXT

Jesus is rebuking them neither for their 'hot' enthusiasm nor their 'cold' antagonism but their 'lukewarm' indifference or indecision. The gift of salvation requires radical obedience. Here is the only place that lukewarm is used. However, the possibility of repentance is still offered vv.18-20.

Spiritually the church is poor, blind, and naked, and not all the banks, pharmacies and looms in Laodicea can provide for its need . . . Of this church alone, the heavenly scrutineer has nothing good to say . . .

So often misapplied to evangelism or a call to salvation, here the LORD is addressing the church: Jesus stands knocking, not with the timid tap that requests admission, but with the imperious hammering of the divine initiative, loud enough to penetrate even the deaf ears of Laodicea. [1]

The water was piped in from Hierapolis. The city also had a signature water problem. It had no water source of its own but had to pipe water in from the hot medicinal springs of Hierapolis.

1. Caird, *Commentary on the Revelation of Saint John the Divine.*

Unfortunately, by the time it arrived there, its tepidness and mineral content made the water nauseating . . . People were prone to spit it from their mouths.[2]

COMMENTARY

This metaphor for ineffectiveness has been linked to the region's water supply. The 'hot' springs of Hierapolis were famous for their medicinal properties and the 'cold' waters of Colossae were prized for their purity. The tepid waters of Laodicea, however, provided neither healing for the spiritually sick nor refreshment for the spiritually weary, were both abundant and bad.[3]

REFLECTIONS

I want to be on fire for Jesus, full of the life and power of His Holy Spirit.

I really couldn't face the prospect of making Him sick of me.

2. Blount, *Revelation*.
3. *Harper's Bible Commentary Society of Biblical Literature* New York 1988

APPLICATIONS

Thank You!

The destiny that the LORD has put upon my life is to enable other people to fulfil their potential. So, I am grateful that you have engaged with this book.

I pray that Jesus will continue to help you as you enjoy His presence through His living word.

I would love to continue our conversation:

dsimlewin@aol.com
+44 (0) 7989 453 612

Bibliography

Achtemeier, Elizabeth. *Nahum – Malachi*. Louisville, KY: Westminster/John Knox, 1988.

Aitken, Kenneth. *Proverbs*. Louisville, KY: Westminster/John Knox, 1986.

Barclay, William. *Mark*. Louisville, KY: Westminster/John Knox, 2017.

——— *Romans*. London: St Andrew, 2010.

Beare, F.W. *Philippians*. Glasgow: Harper Collins, 1987.

Best, Ernest. *1 Peter – New Century Bible Commentary*. Grand Rapids, MI: Eerdemans, 1982.

Bird, Michael. *Colossians and Philemon : A New Covenant Commentary*. Cambridge: Lutterworth, 2009.

Bligh, John. *Galatians*. London: St Paul, 1969.

Blount, Brian. *Revelation*. Louisville, KY: Westminster/John Knox, 2013

Bock, Darrell. *Luke*. Ada, MI: Baker, 1996.

Boring, M. Eugene. *Mark*. London: Presbyterian, 2006.

Brown, Raymond. *Message of Hebrews*. London: IVP, 2021.

Brown, Raymond, et al. *New Jerome Biblical Commentary*. London: Geoffrey Chapman, 1989.

Bruce, F.F. *Epistles of John*. London: Kingsley, 2018

Bruce, F.F., et al. *International Bible Commentary*. Grand Rapids, MI: Zondervan, 1986. Prod ID: FFB-Epistles of John/Pub. Kingsley Books/ Author: F. F. Bruce;

Brueggermann, Walter. *Genesis*. Louisville, KY: Westminster/John Knox, 2010.

Caird, G.B. *Commentary on the Revelation of Saint John the Divine*. London: Bloomsbury, 1985.

Calvin, John. *The Gospel According to St. John*. Bibliolife, 2012.

Carson, D.A., et al. *New Bible Commentary* London: IVP, 1994.

Clowney, Edmund. *Message of 1 Peter*. London: IVP, 2014.

Cohick, Lynn. *A New Covenant Commentary*. Cambridge: Lutterworth, 2013.

Covey, Stephen. *7 Habits of Highly Effective People*. London: Simon & Shuster, 2020 .

Dodd, C.H. *Johannine Epistles*. London: Hodder & Stoughton, 1966.

Eaton, Michael. *1,2,3 John*. Tain, Scotland: Christian Focus, 2005.

Ellicott, Charles. *Commentary on the Whole Bible vol.2*. Eugene, OR: Wipf and Stock, 2015.

Finney, Charles. in 20 *Centuries of Great Preaching vol. XII.* edited by W. Pinson. Santa Ana, CA: W Group, 1974.

Foster, Richard, et al. *Renovaré Spiritual Formation Bible.* San Francisco, CA: Harper Collins, 2005.

Fowl, Stephen. *Philippians.* Grand Rapids, MI: Eerdemans, 2005.

Gardner, Paul. *Ephesians.* Tain, Scotland: Christian Focus 2007.

Graham, Billy. in 20 *Centuries of Great Preaching vol. XII.* edited by W. Pinson. Santa Ana, CA: W Group, 1974.

Guzik, David. *Hebrews.* Santa Barbara, CA: Enduring Word, 2013.

Hamilton, Victor. *Book of Genesis chs.* 1–17. Grand Rapids, MI: Eerdemans, 1996.

Hamlin, E. John. *Joshua.* Grand Rapids, MI: Eerdemans, 1996.

Harrison, R.K. *Leviticus.* London: IVP, 1980.

Henry, Matthew. *Commentary to the Whole Bible in One Volume.* Peabody, MA: Hendrickson, 2008, and

The New Matthew Henry Commentary. edited by Manser, Martin. Grand Rapids, MI: Zondervan, 2010, and

https://www.biblestudytools.com/commentaries/matthew-henry-complete/

Jarvis, Cynthia and Johnson, E. Elizabeth. *Feasting on the Gospels – Matthew, vol.* 1. Louisville, KY: Westminster/John Knox, 2013.

Kanagaraj, Jey. *Gospel of John.* Eugene, OR: Cascade, 2013.

Keck, Leander. *Interpreter's Bible Commentary.* Nashville, TN: Abingdon, 2015.

Keil, C.F. and Delitzch, Franz. *Commentary on the Old Testament.* Peabody, MA: Hendrickson, 2020.

Kelly, J.N.D. *Epistles of Peter and Jude.* London: Bloomsbury, 1969.

Knox, Ronald. *Holy Bible.* North Oil City, PA: Baronius, 2012.

Kroeger, Catherine and Evans, Mary. *Women's Bible Commentary.* London: IVP, 2001.

Leaney, A.R.C. *Letters of Peter and Jude.* Cambridge: Cambridge University Press, 2008.

Lewis, C.S. 'On Forgiveness' in *The Weight of Glory.* Grand Rapids, MI: Zondervan, 2001.

Life Application Study Bible. Carol Stream, IL: Tyndale House, 2020,

Listening to God – Eight Weeks with John. 1984.

Lloyd Jones, D. Martyn. *Romans – Exposition of* 2:1–3:20. Edinburgh: Banner of Truth, 1989.

Longenecker, Richard. *Galatians.* Nashville, TN: Thomas Nelson, 1990.

Luther, Martin. *The Collected Works of Martin Luther.* Charleston, SC: BiblioBazaar, 2007

Maclaren, Alexander. *Expositions of Holy Scriptures : Acts.* New York, NY: Wentworth, 2019.

McKenna, David. *Communicator's Commentary: Job.* Glasgow: W Group, 1986.

Miller, James. *Joshua.* Cambridge: Cambridge University Press, 1974.

Miller, Patrick. *Deuteronomy.* Louisville, KY: Westminster/John Knox, 2011.

Muddiman, John. *Epistle to Ephesians.* London: Baker, 2006.

Newsom, Carol. *Daniel.* Louisville, TN: Westminster John Knox, 2014.
Niditch, Susan. *Judges.* Louisville, TN: Westminster John Knox, 2003.
Oswalt, John. *Book of Isaiah* 1–39. Grand Rapids, MI: Eerdemans, 1998.
Packer, J.I. *In God's Presence: Daily Devotions.* London: Shaw, 2000.
Pawson, David. *Is John* 3:16 *The Gospel?* Reading: Anchor Recordings, 2014.
——— *Unlocking the Bible.* Glasgow: Collins, 2007.
Payne, David. *Deuteronomy.* Westminster/John Knox, 1985.
Peake, A. *Commentary on the Bible.* London: Nelson, 1962.
Plantinga-Pauw, Amy. *Proverbs and Ecclesiastes.* Louisville, KY: Westminster/ John Knox, 2015.
Pope Francis. *Angelus Address Laetare Sunday - A Time to Rejoice.* March 11, 2018.
Robertson, O. Palmer *Books of Nahum, Habakkuk and Zephaniah.* Grand Rapids, MI: Eerdemans, 1994..
Stott, John. *Letters of John.* London: IVP, 2020
——— *The Cross.* London: IVP, 2009.
Watts, John. *Isaiah.* Grand Rapids, MI: Zondervan, 2020.
Witherington, Ben. *Acts of the Apostles.* Grand Rapids, MI: Eerdemans, 2001.

www.ingramcontent.com/pod-product-compliance
Lightning Source LLC
LaVergne TN
LVHW010933100826
845153LV00001B/15
9781666724929